A Study in Hebrews
Israel and the New Covenant

Hebrews 8:1-2 (KJV)

[1] Now of the things which we have spoken *this is* the sum: We have such an high priest, who is set on the right hand of the throne of the Majesty in the heavens; [2] A minister of the sanctuary, and of the true tabernacle, which the Lord pitched, and not man.

A Study in Hebrews
Israel and the New Covenant
Author M J Tiry
Copyright 2024 M. J. Tiry

Because of the dynamic nature of the internet, any web addresses or links contained in this book may have changed since publication and may no longer be valid. The views expressed in this work are solely those of the author.

All scripture references in this book are taken from the King James Version of the Bible.

ISBN: 979-8-9903305-6-6. Paper
ISBN: 979-8-9903305-7-3 Hard Cover
ISBN: 979-8-9903305-8-0 eBook

Library of Congress Control Number: 2024918562

Print Information Available on the Last Page

DEDICATION

Dedicated: This study is dedicated to the students of the Word of God who have learned to love the study of the Word of truth rightly divided. It has been my greatest joy in life to fellowship with such students, and I greatly appreciate the studies of others that opened the Word of God to my understanding. The following study notes are in part an effort to present an exposé of the text of the Book of Hebrews and to compare Scripture with Scripture to convey to other students the two-fold purpose of God in our Lord Jesus Christ. As always, this is presented with the note of exhortation and warning to test any and all teaching as in Acts 17:11 and receive the Word with all readiness of mind and search the Scriptures to see if those things are so

CONTENTS

List of Tables

Outline of Hebrews

Part I   The Great Salvation
1.   The Son better than the prophets (1:1-3)
2.   The Son better than the angels (1:1-4)
3.   Parenthesis: **Warning** (2:1-4)
4.   The earth put under the man (2:5-8)
5.   Man made lower than the angels but will be above them in Christ (2:9-18)

Part II   The Rest of God (3:1-4:16)
1.   Christ the Son better than Moses the servant (3:1-6)
2.   Exhortation to enter that rest (3:7-19)
3.   There is a better rest for the believer (4:1-8)
4.   Believer's rest in the perfect work of redemption (4:9-13)
5.   The believer kept in perfect rest by mercy and grace in the Son (4:14-19)

Part III   Israel's Great High Priest
1.   The office of the high priest (5:1-4)
2.   Christ a Priest after the Order of Melchisedec (5:5-10)
3.   Parenthesis: **Warning** (5:11-6:12)
4.   The High Priest is within the veil (6:13-20)
5.   The Historic Melchisedec is a type of Christ (7:1-3)
6.   Melchisedec's priesthood greater than Aaron's (7:4-8:6)
   a.   Aaron paid tithes in Abraham
   b.   Aaron's priesthood made nothing perfect
   c.   Aaron's priests died but Christ ever liveth
   d.   Aaron's priests served the shadow but Christ is the substance
   e.   Christ mediates a better covenant

Part IV   The New Covenant better than the old (8:7-10:39)
1.   Ordinances of the Old Covenant were just types (9:1-10)
2.   The Sanctuary and Sacrifices of the New are Realities (9:11-15)
3.   The New Covenant Sealed with better blood (9:16-22)
4.   The Heavenly Sanctuary is purged with a better sacrifice (9:23-24)
5.   The One sacrifice of the new replaces the many of the old (9:25-10:18)
6.   Believers worship is in the Holiest (10:19-26)
7.   Parenthesis **Warning** (10:26-39)

Part V   The Superiority of Faith (11:1-40)
1.   The Sphere of Faith (11:1-3)
2.   Examples of Faith
   a.   Abel
   b.   Enoch
   c.   Noah
   d.   Abraham and Sarah
   e.   Isaac and Jacob
   f.   Joseph
   g.   Moses and his parents
   h.   Joshua
   i.   Rahab
   j.   Et. al.

Part VI   Walk and Worship of the Believing Hebrews
1.   Jesus' Example (12:1&2)
2.   Parenthesis: **Warning** (12:3-17)
   a.   The Father's Chastening (12:3-15)
   b.   Esau as an example of failure in faith (12-:16)
3.   The Hebrew believers do not come to Sinai
4.   **Warnings** and Instructions (12:25-13:9)
5.   Separation and Worship (13:10-14)

6. The believer's sacrifice (13:15&16)
7. The believer's obedience (13:17)

Abbreviations used:

c.	circa ("about/Approximately")
cp	Compare
e.g.	exampligratia ("for example")
et. al.	Et allii ("and others")
etc.	Et. cetara ("and so forth")
ff	and the following (verses, pages, etc.)
i.e.	id. est. (that is)
vas, vv	verse (s)
viz.	Videlicet ('namely")

ACKNOWLEDGMENTS

Thank you: I give thanks to my daughters Leah and Anna who helped me with the formatting and to my daughter Charissa who helped me with the illustrations. Special thanks to my daughter Naomi for her help in the publishing process. I give thanks also to Letty Rasmussen, Vince Kison, and Heather McKeen who provided the proof reading of this document. I give thanks to my dear wife Linda whose patience allowed me to devote time to this effort and who shares the appreciation for the need of such a work

Notes to the Reader:

A word is in order here on how to study the Bible and actually how to approach the Bible. Some basic principles to hold in our study of Scripture then are:

1. All of scripture came from the mouth of God and it fully equips the man of God to do anything that God would have him do. "All scripture *is* given by inspiration of God, and *is* profitable for doctrine, for reproof, for correction, for instruction in righteousness: That the man of God may be perfect, throughly furnished unto all good works." (2 Timothy 3:16-17) It can be said that the Holy Spirit never works apart from the Bible and the Bible never works apart from the Holy Spirit.

2. The term "inspiration of God" in 2Timothy 3:16 means that it was breathe out of God's mouth. It is truly as the Lord tells the devil in Matthew 4:4 "It is written; Man shall not live by bread alone, but by every word that proceedeth out of the mouth of God." And that is the origin of every word of scripture – from the mouth of God.

3. Scripture must be studied in its context in order for it to make sense. There are two contexts: the immediate context in which the passage is set and there is the remote context that looks at the Bible as a whole. Billy Sunday is said to have made the statement "A text without a context is a pretext." That concept is what Peter is communicating when he said in 2Peter 1:20 & 21 "Knowing this first, that no prophecy of the scripture is of any private interpretation. For the prophecy came not in old time by the will of man: but holy men of God spake *as they were* moved by the Holy Ghost." No passage of scripture is intended to stand by itself but rather each passage actually relates to every other passage of scripture. One of the greatest tools to Bible study is a good cross reference (One that I like is The Treasury of Scripture Knowledge). By comparing scripture with scripture the Bible teaches itself. The Bible itself is its greatest and best teacher.

4. While all of scripture is written for our learning, not every passage of scripture is addressed to us. The word of truth then must be rightly divided. Paul tells us this in 2Timothy 2:15 saying "Study to shew thyself approved unto God, a workman that needeth not to be ashamed, rightly dividing the word of truth." We trust that appendix 4 of this book will be very helpful in seeing this concept.

5. Another key to understanding the Bible is simply to let it say what it clearly says. It is a major mistake to spiritualize scripture. The Bible is written to be taken literally. There are times when the Bible uses figures of speech (figurative language) but when it does it is apparent that such is the case. Basically, we must remember the adage "if the literal sense makes perfect sense, seek no other sense."

6. God has taken great care to give us His inspired word and gave it without error. He has also pledged to preserve it so. (Psalm 12:6-7) "The words of the LORD *are* pure words: *as* silver tried in a furnace of earth, purified seven times. Thou shalt keep them, O LORD, thou shalt preserve them from this generation for ever." It is the conviction of this author that there exists today a preserved text of the inspired and inerrant Word of God. This is not in the originals for they have been lost through time but this preservation of scripture is in the multiplicity of copies. It was God's desire and design that the Bible gets into the hands of the people. If there is a doctrine of preservation, then that preservation is done in the multiplicity of copies. This author holds the conviction that the preserved text line is the Received Text (Majority Text) of the New Testament and the Masoretic Text of the Hebrew Old Testament. Since there is only one translation in print in English today from these, all scripture references in this study are from the King James Bible.

7. There is yet another key to an effective study of the word of God. That is the heart attitude of the Bereans of Acts 17:11. They received the Word with and open mind but they did not just take any man's word for truth or error of what was said until they searched it out in the scripture. That approach gave them protection from error for they made the Word of God their final authority and examined what everyone said based on the Word of Truth – the Bible.

8. Each chapter in this study has a set of study guide questions. The answers to these can be found in sequential order in the corresponding chapter. Those who are taking this as a study course are encouraged to have the study questions in front of them and write the answers as they encounter them in the text.

9. One final thing regarding the Bible having the impact in our lives that God intended it to have is the simple matter of believing it. Paul tells the Thessalonians that they received the word of God, they received it not as the word of men but as it is in truth the word of God, which "...effectually worketh in you that believe." It is not just

the understanding of it that makes it effective but applying it by faith to one's life that makes it effective to give spiritual strength and vitality.

10. The author has a series of four books in what is called the Prophecy Series. This book is the third in the series. The first in the series is *"A Study in Daniel – The King and the Kingdom in Prophecy."* The second of this series is *"Matthew's Gospel- Study of the King and His Kingdom."* The fourth and last in the series is *"A Study in the Revelation—the End Times Fulfillment of Bible Prophecy."*

INTRODUCTION TO HEBREWS

The Book of Hebrews speaks of Christ as the Apostle and High Priest of Israel. (Heb. 3:1). An apostle is literally "one sent." Our Lord Jesus Christ is today the Head of the Church which is His Body – a Gentile Church. That is how He is presented in the Pauline Epistles of Romans through Philemon. However, in the four Gospel accounts we find that He was not sent but to the House of Israel (Matt. 10:6; 15:24). In the books of Hebrews through the Revelation, we find that He is sent to Israel to be her High Priest. That is, He is the one to represent Israel before God the Father. There are 12 apostles under Him in that capacity (Matt. 19:28). In fact Israel, from the outset of God's call of the nation, was to be a "Kingdom of Priests." Note God's words to Israel in Exodus 19:5-6 -- "⁵ Now therefore, if ye will obey my voice indeed, and keep my covenant, then ye shall be a peculiar treasure unto me above all people: for all the earth *is* mine: ⁶ And ye shall be unto me a kingdom of priests, and an holy nation. These *are* the words which thou shalt speak unto the children of Israel."

We understand that the function of a priest is to represent a third party before God. We see that the nation of Israel was to represent the Gentiles before God when the promised kingdom is established. Jesus Christ, after His resurrection and ascension back to heaven, commissions the twelve apostles who will one day sit on twelve thrones judging the twelve tribes of Israel (Matt. 19:28) to proclaim the Gospel of the Kingdom. Their commission was to proclaim *the gospel of the kingdom of heaven* in all of the world beginning at Jerusalem. We see the strategy that He lays out for them in His parting words to them in Acts 1:6-9 "⁶ When they therefore were come together, they asked of him, saying, Lord, wilt thou at this time restore again the kingdom to Israel? ⁷ And he said unto them, It is not for you to know the times or the seasons, which the Father hath put in his own power. ⁸ But ye shall receive power, after that the Holy Ghost is come upon you: and ye shall be witnesses unto me both in Jerusalem, and in all Judaea, and in Samaria, and unto the uttermost part of the earth. ⁹ And when he had spoken these things, while they beheld, he was taken up; and a cloud received him out of their sight."

What we see in the four gospel accounts and in the first seven chapters of the Book of Acts is a three step process by which God appealed to Israel to trust Jesus Christ as her Messiah and thus God would set up His Kingdom of priests as a Holy nation and a royal priesthood. Note Peter's words to that effect in 1Peter as he addresses the believing remnant of the nation.

"⁴ To whom coming, *as unto* a living stone, disallowed indeed of men, but chosen of God, *and* precious, ⁵ Ye also, as lively stones [living stones], are built up a spiritual house, an holy priesthood, to offer up spiritual sacrifices [on behalf of the Gentiles], acceptable to God by [under the authority of] Jesus Christ. ⁶ Wherefore also it is contained in the scripture, Behold, I lay in Sion a chief corner stone, elect, precious: and he that believeth on him shall not be confounded. ⁷ Unto you therefore which believe *he is* precious: but unto them which be disobedient, the stone which the builders disallowed, the same is made the head of the corner, ⁸ And a stone of stumbling, and a rock of offence, *even to them* which stumble at the word, being disobedient: whereunto also they were appointed. ⁹ But ye *are* a chosen generation, a royal priesthood, an holy nation, a peculiar people; that ye should shew forth the praises of him who hath called you out of darkness into his marvelous light: ¹⁰ Which in time past *were* not a people, but *are* now the people of God: which had not obtained mercy, but now have obtained mercy. ¹¹ Dearly beloved, I beseech *you* as strangers and pilgrims, abstain from fleshly lusts, which war against the soul; ¹² Having your conversation honest among the Gentiles: that, whereas they speak against you as evildoers, they may by *your* good works, which they shall behold, glorify God in the day of visitation [when Jesus returns to set up His Kingdom]." **1Peter 2:4-12 (KJV)**

In order to understand the Book of Hebrews and to see where it fits into God's plan for the establishing of the kingdom, we need to follow the unfolding of the events that pertain to the offer of the kingdom to Israel. It was a three step process because it was a threefold appeal that God made to the nation. Through the ministry of John the Baptist, the Father appeals to them to repent and change their minds about what their purpose as a nation actually was. John was sent by the Father (John 1:33) to practice the cleansing rite of water baptism as "The baptism of repentance for the remission of sins…" The purpose for John's ministry was to bring Israel to repentance so that the Messiah can come to a clean nation.

If one should wonder where John got the idea of the water rite for cleansing, one needs to go to the Old Testament and the ordinance of the red heifer in Numbers 19. There is a misconception that many have in studying John's ministry that he started something new with water baptism. In fact, we can understand from the questions raised of John in John 1:25 "Why baptizest thou then if thou be not that Christ, nor Elias, neither that prophet?" that Israel fully expected water baptism to be associated with the offer of the coming kingdom.

When John tells the inquirers sent from the scribes and Pharisees "He that sent me to baptize with water…," he was referring to the Father who was sending John as the fore runner of His only begotten Son to introduce Him to Israel. "[33] And I knew him not: but he that sent me to baptize with water, the same said unto me, Upon whom thou shalt see the Spirit descending, and remaining on him, the same is he which baptizeth with the Holy Ghost." (John 1:33) We see then that it was the Father who makes the first appeal to the nation to ready its heart for the coming kingdom of heaven.

The Kingdom of Heaven verses Dispensation of Grace

"Then shall the King say unto them on his right hand, Come, ye blessed of my Father, inherit the kingdom prepared for you from the foundation of the world:" (Matthew 25:34)

From the very foundation of the world, God had in mind that kingdom that He would establish on this earth. These words were spoken by our Lord Jesus Christ at the close of His earthly ministry. The context is Matthew 25:31-46 where we see the Lord speaking prophetically of judging the Gentile nations after the close of the Tribulation Period. The believing Gentiles in this context would be called to go into the promised Kingdom of Heaven when the entire world would be blessed through Abraham's multiplied seed – the redeemed nation of Israel. This would be the fulfillment of the Abrahamic Covenant. We will study more on that covenant later. What is significant about this statement is that the Kingdom was in God's mind "…from the foundation of the world." In fact, all of what He had done up to that point in history was for the purpose of establishing that kingdom in the earth.

The term "the Kingdom of Heaven" is used 32 times in Matthew's gospel but nowhere else in the Bible. It is a reference to the kingdom that will be set up on the earth when Jesus Christ returns to the earth at the close of the coming Tribulation period. Under that kingdom, this earth will have its finest hour under the reign of Jesus Christ. Jesus will reign over redeemed Israel and Israel will reign over the earth. Israel will be under the New Covenant by which the nation will finally be in such a state that she will be the means whereby Abraham's seed can truly be a blessing to the Gentile world.

What is missed by much of Christianity today is the fact that this promised kingdom was actually officially offered to the nation Israel in the first chapters of the Book of Acts. The sin of blaspheming the Holy Ghost that the Lord spoke of in Matthew Chapter 12 verses 31 and 32 occurred as He (the Holy Spirit) witnessed to that nation through

Peter and the twelve apostles at Pentecost. Israel's final and official rejection of Jesus Christ as her Messiah did not occur with the rejection of John's ministry (Matt. 21:24-27) nor did it occur when the nation, through her leaders, demanded that Jesus be crucified (Matt. 27:22). Rather, that final rejection occurred in the Book of Acts when the nation rejected the resurrected Christ as her Messiah. The nation committed the unpardonable sin by rejecting the call to Israel made by the Holy Ghost through the twelve apostles at Pentecost in Acts Chapters 2 through 7. That was the third of a threefold appeal that God made to the nation.

The Father's Appeal
Let's consider those three appeals to Israel regarding the Kingdom of Heaven. The first appeal to Israel regarding the kingdom of heaven came with the ministry of John the Baptist.

> "1 In those days came John the Baptist, preaching in the wilderness of Judaea, 2 And saying, Repent ye: for the kingdom of heaven is at hand. 3 For this is he that was spoken of by the prophet Esaias, saying, The voice of one crying in the wilderness, Prepare ye the way of the Lord, make his paths straight." (Matthew 3:1-3)

We note from John 1:32-33 that it was the Father that sent John to appeal to Israel.

> [32] And John bare record, saying, I saw the Spirit descending from heaven like a dove, and it abode upon him. [33] And I knew him not: but he that sent me to baptize with water, the same said unto me, Upon whom thou shalt see the Spirit descending, and remaining on him, the same is he which baptizeth with the Holy Ghost. [34] And I saw, and bare record that this is the Son of God.(John 1:32-34)

This appeal by John the Baptist is actually God the Father's call to Israel to get ready for her Messiah. The passage actually sets the course for the four gospel accounts of our Lord's earthly ministry. The issue was a kingdom that is called "The Kingdom of Heaven." The kingdom in view here is not to be understood as a kingdom in heaven. This Kingdom was to be set up upon the earth. His kingdom will be set up on earth by the God of Heaven. Matthew's gospel is the account of our Lord's earthly ministry in which He is presented as the seed of David who will sit on the Throne of David in that Kingdom that was promised in the Old Testament Scriptures. We see it described in Daniel 2:44.

> "And in the days of these kings shall the God of heaven set up a kingdom, which shall never be destroyed: and the kingdom shall not be left to other people, but it shall break in pieces and consume all these kingdoms, and it shall stand for ever." (Daniel 2:44)

That kingdom will be called the "Kingdom of Heaven" not only because the God of Heaven sets it up but also because, when it is set up, God's will is going to be done on earth as it is in heaven. Note the words in what is called the Lord's Prayer: "After this manner therefore pray ye: Our Father which art in heaven, Hallowed be thy name. Thy kingdom come, Thy will be done in earth, as it is in heaven." (Matthew 6:9-10)

> **The Son's Appeal**
> After John is put in prison, the Lord Himself takes up the call to Israel. We saw the appeal of the Father and here we see it made by Jesus Christ, the only begotten Son, to Israel.

> "12 Now when Jesus had heard that John was cast into prison, he departed into Galilee; 13 And leaving Nazareth,

he came and dwelt in Capernaum, which is upon the sea coast, in the borders of Zabulon and Nephthalim: 14 That it might be fulfilled which was spoken by Esaias the prophet, saying,15 The land of Zabulon, and the land of Nephthalim, by the way of the sea, beyond Jordan, Galilee of the Gentiles; 16 The people which sat in darkness saw great light; and to them which sat in the region and shadow of death light is sprung up. 17 *From that time Jesus began to preach, and to say, Repent: for the kingdom of heaven is at hand.*" (Matthew 4:12-17 emphasis added)

The Appeal of the Disciples

In the first ten chapters of Matthew's Gospel we see the calling out of the twelve disciples who become the twelve apostles. They then continue the appeal to the nation to repent because the Kingdom of Heaven is at hand. "At hand" meaning that it is ready to be set up. Note that they were not to go to the Gentiles or even to the Samaritans but only to the house of Israel. They were sent out with supernatural powers to demonstrate that this was a serious call by God to Israel.

"5 These twelve Jesus sent forth, and commanded them, saying, Go not into the way of the Gentiles, and into any city of the Samaritans enter ye not: 6 But go rather to the lost sheep of the house of Israel. 7 And as ye go, preach, saying, *The kingdom of heaven is at hand.* 8 Heal the sick, cleanse the lepers, raise the dead, cast out devils: freely ye have received, freely give. 9 Provide neither gold, nor silver, nor brass in your purses, 10 Nor scrip for your journey, neither two coats, neither shoes, nor yet staves: for the workman is worthy of his meat. (Matthew 10:5-10 emphasis added)

The Appeal by the Holy Ghost

After the death, burial and resurrection of our Lord, He again sends the twelve after His ascension with still the same message. The only difference now is that it is the Holy Ghost now calling to the nation to repent of their sin of unbelief. To repent was to change their mind about who this Jesus of Nazareth really is – to change their mind and repent of their deed of having crucified their Messiah. Note Peter's word to that effect:

"12 And when Peter saw it, he answered unto the people, Ye men of Israel, why marvel ye at this? or why look ye so earnestly on us, as though by our own power or holiness we had made this man to walk? 13 The God of Abraham, and of Isaac, and of Jacob, the God of our fathers, hath glorified his Son Jesus; whom ye delivered up, and denied him in the presence of Pilate, when he was determined to let him go. 14 But ye denied the Holy One and the Just, and desired a murderer to be granted unto you; 15 And killed the Prince of life, whom God hath raised from the dead; whereof we are witnesses. 16 And his name through faith in his name hath made this man strong, whom ye see and know: yea, the faith which is by him hath given him this perfect soundness in the presence of you all. (Acts 3:12-16)

Note that Peter is seeking to bring true conviction on the nation for their deed of having put their Messiah to death. What we must not lose sight of here though is that this is the Holy Ghost's appeal to the nation. Now though, it is a call to trust in the resurrected Christ. Note as he goes on that this is the actual official offer of the kingdom to Israel.

"17 And now, brethren, I wot that through ignorance ye did it, as did also your rulers. 18 But those things, which God before had shewed by the mouth of all his prophets, that Christ should suffer, he hath so fulfilled. 19 Repent ye therefore, and be converted, that your sins may be blotted out, when the times of refreshing shall come from the presence of the Lord; 20 *And he shall send Jesus Christ, which before was preached unto you: 21 Whom the heaven must receive until the times of restitution of all things, which God hath spoken by the mouth of all his holy prophets since the world began.* (Acts 3:17-21 Emphasis added)

Note from this passage what would have happened if Israel would have repented (that is, had they changed their mind about who He really is). Had they as a nation genuinely repented, what would happen?
- Their sins would have been blotted out when Christ returned to earth (which would have happened shortly thereafter to establish the kingdom). This would have been Israel's official Day of Atonement. We Gentiles today individually receive the atonement the moment that we believe that Jesus died for our sins (Romans 5:11). Israel (the believing remnant of the nation) will receive their atonement as a nation at their real Day of Atonement when Jesus returns to set up His kingdom.
- God would send Jesus Christ back to earth to set up the kingdom
- God will then restore to Israel all of things that He had spoken by the mouth of all His holy Prophets since the world began.

Now let's draw our attention to verse 23. "And it shall come to pass that every soul, which will not hear that prophet, *shall be destroyed from among the people.*" (Acts 3:23 emphasis added). This is what John had warned Israel about in Matthew 3:11 and 12

"I [John] indeed baptize you [Israel] with water unto repentance: but he that cometh after me [Jesus] is mightier than I, whose shoes I am not worthy to bear: he shall baptize you [Israel] with the Holy Ghost, and with fire [of judgment]. 12 Whose fan *is* in his hand, and he will throughly purge his floor [the nation at large], *and gather his wheat into the garner; but he will burn up the chaff [unbelievers] with unquenchable fire.*" (Emphasis added)

The meaning of this purging of His floor is made clear by what John said in verse 10 "And now the axe is laid unto the root of the trees: every tree which bringeth not forth good fruit is hewn down, and cast into the fire." This is serious business. The trees here are Israelites. All of Israel will be saved when the kingdom is set up (Romans 11:26). That does not mean that God will somehow force unbelievers to believe and be faithful. It means that those who will not believe of their own free will are going to be purged from the nation. Only believing faithful Israelites will go into that Kingdom and the New Covenant will take effect through them.

The fire in verses 10 and 12 of Matthew 3 is the Gehenna fire that we see described in Deuteronomy 32:22 and Matthew 10:28. Ultimately the purpose for the Tribulation Period is to purge unbelief from Israel and to get Israel saved as a nation. The apostle talks about this in Romans 11:26 and 27 saying "And so all Israel shall be saved: as it is written, There shall come out of Sion the Deliverer, and shall turn away ungodliness from Jacob: For this is my covenant unto them, when I shall take away their sins."

This witness of the Holy Ghost takes us back to what the Lord told the unbelieving scribes and Pharisees in Matthew 12: 31 and 32

"31 Wherefore I say unto you, All manner of sin and blasphemy shall be forgiven unto men: but the blasphemy against the Holy Ghost shall not be forgiven unto men. 32 And whosoever speaketh a word against the Son of man, it shall be forgiven him: but whosoever speaketh against the Holy Ghost, it shall not be forgiven him, neither in this world, neither in the world to come.

The nation's rejection of the message from the Father given through John did not result in them being set aside nor did their rejection of the witness of the Son in Matthew Chapter 12. However, when they reject the witness of the Holy Ghost, (which did not come until Pentecost in the Book of Acts) things will change.

The Holy Spirit's Appeal to Israel and Stephen's Indictment of Israel

From Peter's message in Acts Chapter 3 to Stephen's message in Chapter 7 of Acts, it is the Holy Ghost witnessing to Israel that the one Israel crucified is the nation's Messiah. However, Israel had an opportunity to repent of that deed until they stoned Stephen. Had they done so, the Tribulation period would have followed and run its course and then the kingdom would have been established. Let's consider Stephen's pointed message to Israel:

> "51 Ye stiffnecked and uncircumcised in heart and ears, *ye do always resist the Holy Ghost:* as your fathers did, so do ye. 52 Which of the prophets have not your fathers persecuted? and they have slain them which shewed before of the coming of the Just One; of whom ye have been now the betrayers and murderers: 53 Who have received the law by the disposition of angels, and have not kept it." (Acts 7:51-53 emphasis added)

Stephen brought the indictment against the leaders of Israel. What Stephen sees as he looked up into heaven and what happened next is most significant to the rest of the Book of Acts and for life on earth for centuries to come after that. Note the next verse:

> "55 But he, being full of the Holy Ghost, looked up stedfastly into heaven, and saw the glory of God, and Jesus standing on the right hand of God, 56 And said, Behold, I see the heavens opened, and the Son of man standing on the right hand of God." (Acts 7:55-56)

Stephen sees Jesus standing at the right hand of God in heaven. This posture is significant because of what we read in Acts 2:32 from Peter's statement to the Israel:

> "32 This Jesus hath God raised up, whereof we all are witnesses. 33 Therefore being by the right hand of God exalted, and having received of the Father the promise of the Holy Ghost, he hath shed forth this, which ye now see and hear. 34 For David is not ascended into the heavens: but he saith himself, The LORD said unto my Lord, *Sit thou on my right hand, 35 Until I make thy foes thy footstool.* 36 Therefore let all the house of Israel know assuredly, that God hath made that same Jesus, whom ye have crucified, both Lord and Christ." (Acts 2:32-36 Emphasis added)

Israel's Time to Repent was up

Jesus was to sit until it was time for the Father to make His enemies His footstool. So what was to happen at this point?

The Seven Year Tribulation (the seventieth week of Daniel Chapter 9) was to come.

Israel was to be purged of unbelief by the Tribulation Period.

Armageddon would have happened at the culmination of the Seventieth week.

Jesus would have returned to establish the kingdom.

But! That is not what happened. What did happen?

Jesus Saves Saul of Tarsus.

Jesus Reveals the Mystery through Paul concerning the Dispensation of the Grace of the God that we live in today.

Jesus temporarily sets Israel aside to reconcile the world (Rom. 11:15). This reconciling made the whole world savable apart from Israel.

All of the wonderful blessings that the world will enjoy in the promised kingdom have been postponed for over at least 1980 years so far.

Most importantly, God started forming a new elect agency through which He will work in the world. He started the church the Body of Christ – what is essentially a Gentile church.

An Un-prophesied and Unprecedented Change in the Geopolitics of the World

The offer of the Kingdom to Israel was withdrawn with the saving of Saul of Tarsus. The stark reality of this is the fact that God does not have His Nation on earth today. Rather, what the apostle calls "this present evil world" began (Galatians 1:4). For nearly 2000 years now there is no nation on earth that could claim to be God's nation. Israel could have been and should have been that nation -- but that is a lost opportunity (at least temporarily). All of the blessings that the world will experience under the kingdom reign of Jesus Christ are temporarily held in abeyance.

However, though God does not have His nation in the earth today; He does have His people on earth. God did something totally un-prophesied and unprecedented. He interrupted His program and His dealings with His nation of Israel and set that nation aside as the elect agency by which He works in the world. Instead, He started a new and different elect agency. He started a Gentile church. This Gentile church is called out from the Gentile masses -- which now includes Israel for that nation is today regarded by God as just another Gentile nation.

The wonderful blessed truth is that the church which is Christ's Body is composed of all who come to faith in the redeeming work that Jesus Christ accomplished on the cross whether they be Jew or Gentile. All who come in faith are "justified freely by his grace through the redemption that is in Christ Jesus: Whom God hath set forth to be a propitiation through faith in his blood, to declare his righteousness for the remission of sins that are past, through the forbearance of God; To declare, I say at this time his righteousness: that he might be just and the justifier of him which believeth in Jesus." (Romans 3: 24 – 26). This justification is apart from the deeds of the Law – which has now been taken out of the way. Lest any should miss the glory and wonder of it, let's understand that today anyone can have their sins forgiven and be reckoned by God as righteous (fit to be in God's presence) by simple faith in the good news that Christ died for our sins according to the scriptures, and was buried and rose again the third day according to the scriptures (1Corinthians 15:1-3). When a person believes that simple message, that person is baptized by the Holy Ghost into the Body of Christ (1Cor. 12:12 – 13) and sealed to eternal life (Eph. 1:13; 4:30).

The Church which is Christ's Body is the subject of the body of doctrine that we know of as the Pauline Epistles. It is what Paul calls "the preaching of Jesus Christ according to the revelation of the mystery" (Romans 16:25). In these epistles the body of Christ is presented as if it were a virtual man that has Jesus Christ as the head and the collection of all believers in the world as the body (Eph. 2:15). This one new man actually is at work in the world today to "edify itself in love" (Ephesians 4:15 and 16).

If God does not have a nation in earth today that is His nation, how does He carry on His work of redemption today? He does it through the new agency of believers (the church which is His body) as they individually live the Christian life and more so as they function together in local churches. The local church is what Paul calls "the house of God, the church of the living God, the pillar and ground of the truth." (1Timothy 3:15)

The Mystery concerning the Dispensation of the Grace of God

The information that God has given to us to govern how we who live in the dispensation of grace are to relate to Him is contained in the Pauline Epistles. We today have a relationship to God that is not detailed in any of the covenants of promise that God made with Israel or in the Law of Moses but rather is laid out for us in a body of doctrine called "The preaching of Jesus Christ according to the revelation of the mystery." (Romans 16:25) It is called the mystery because it is "...the hidden wisdom, which God ordained before the world unto our glory..." but was not revealed until the time was right to do so. The time for the revelation of this hidden wisdom came when Israel rejected the offer of the Kingdom in Acts Chapter 7 with the stoning of Stephen. The next event in prophecy after the rejection of the offer of the kingdom should have been the seventieth week of Daniel (or what we call the tribulation period). However, instead of the Lord returning to bring the seventieth week of Daniel Chapter 9, He came to save Saul of Tarsus and to reveal the mystery through him.

There are seven elements to this body of doctrine called the mystery. The Book of Hebrews is the basic book that is the foundational book to the circumcision epistles and to the prophetic program in general. In order for us the get an accurate understanding of the message the Book of Hebrews and where it fits into Gods plan for the ages, we need to first understand the seven elements of the mystery – the body of doctrine that temporarily interrupted prophecy. They are:

1. The Dispensation of Grace - The mystery starts with the beginning of the dispensation of the grace of God in which there is no unpardonable sin. Saul of Tarsus could be forgiven in spite of having committed the unpardonable sin of blaspheming the Holy Ghost because a new dispensation started in which there is no unpardonable sin (Matthew 12:31 and 1Timothy 1:14). Paul tells us that it was through him that Jesus Christ revealed the mystery involving the dispensation of grace (Ephesians 3:3-4; Colossian 1: 26-27).

2. The Present Temporary Partial Blindness of Israel (Romans 11:25): Israel is today in partial blindness because they, as a nation, rejected the offer of the kingdom extended to them in Acts. It is a partial blindness because there are some Israelites getting saved today but they are saved by coming to God as a Gentile would. It is also only temporary because it is a blindness that will last until the fullness of the Gentiles is come in (Romans 11:25). The fullness of the Gentiles is a reference to the completion of the calling out of the Body of Christ. When the church which is His body is complete, it will be removed from earth to heaven. The rapture (the catching away to heaven of the body of Christ -- 1Thessalonians 4:15-17; 1Corinthians 15:51) will close the dispensation of grace and will take the church the Body of Christ to its eternal home in the heavens (2 Corinthians 5:1).

3. The Gospel -- The truth about what was actually accomplished on the cross of Calvary is one of the elements to the mystery revealed by Jesus Christ through Paul. It is what Paul called "the mystery of the gospel for which he was an ambassador in bonds..." (Ephesians 6:19-20). Paul refers to this as "My Gospel" (Romans 2:16; 16:25), the gospel of his Son (Romans 1:9); the gospel of Christ (Romans 1:16); the gospel of peace (Romans 10:15) and the gospel of God (Romans 15:16). This gospel of Calvary is clearly laid out in detail in the Bible first in Romans 3: 20-25. The Book of Romans presents the merits of the cross in the context of this present dispensation of grace. The Book of Hebrews then takes that information and presents it in

the context of Israel's Kingdom program. It is apparent that the writer of Hebrews then got the information about what all was accomplished on Calvary by way of redemption from Paul.

4. The Rapture: The truth concerning the fact that there is now with the church which is Christ's body a new elect agency at work in the world – the church which is Christ's Body (a Gentile church). It is through this new elect agency that God will reconcile the heavenly places to Himself. Involved in this will be a rapture which catches the members of the Body of Christ up to heaven where the individual members will have resurrected (and/or changed) bodies that will be eternal in the heavens (2 Corinthians 5:1). With this addition of this mystery to God's program for the ages, we see how it is "That in the dispensation of the fullness of times he might gather together in one all things in Christ, both which are in heaven and which are on earth…" (Ephesians 1:9 and 10 and Colossians 1:14). After the catching away of the church which is Christ's body to heaven, God will again pick up His dealings with Israel. It will be the portion of the New Testament scripture that we know of as Hebrews through Revelation that will take the nation through the seventieth week of Daniel and into that kingdom. The rapture is more than simply a resurrection. It also includes those members of the body of Christ who are alive on earth when that event happens being caught up and changed so as to have bodies that can live and function there in the heavens. That body that believers will have will be celestial in nature. It will be capable of living and functioning in the heavens where its eternal home will be (1Cor. 15:40).

5. The Great Mystery: This involves the forming of a unique elect agency that is similar to the marriage relationship (Ephesians 5:32) to form the one new man of Ephesians 2:15. This one new man is composed of Jews and Gentiles joined together in one body that is "…flesh of his flesh and bone of his bone…" This one new man is Christ according to the revelation of the mystery. That elect agency is doing the work of the ministry today in the dispensation of grace to reach lost souls. It will be the 144,000 and the remnant of Israel that will do that in the coming tribulation period.

6. The Mystery of Godliness - This one new man comprises the elect agency through which God's character and personality is manifest in the world today. Godliness is manifest in the world today through the church which is Christ's body as it functions in local churches (1Timothy 3:16). Godliness is produced in the church the body of Christ by the work of the Holy Spirit working through the Word of God by means of the process of regeneration (Titus 3:5). Regeneration today is a work of the Holy Spirit that is similar to, but yet different from, the work that the Holy Spirit will do in Israel when the New Covenant will take effect for them in the Kingdom.

7. The Mystery of Iniquity - While God's character and personality is manifest in the church, Satan's character is manifest in the world of the unsaved masses which carries out his plan in the earth (2 Thessalonians 2:7). While the Holy Spirit of God carries on an enlightening ministry in believers (Eph. 1: 9-10), Satan works in the lives of unbelievers to keep them blinded to the truth (Eph. 2:2; 2Cor. 4:4). The working of deception that Satan had in store for Israel in the Tribulation was already at work when God started the dispensation of grace. The church the body of Christ is what restrains it in the world today. It will be the believing remnant of Israel that will do that restraining work during in the coming Tribulation.

The Law – It's past, present, and future roles in man's relationship to God.

The apostle Paul has much to say about the Law in Galatians especially as it relates to us today in the dispensation of grace. Let's look at Galatians Chapter 3 on the law:

> Galatians 3:11-27 (KJV) [11] But that no man is justified by the law in the sight of God, *it is* evident: for, the just shall live by faith. [12] And the law is not of faith: but, The man that doeth them shall live in them. [13] Christ hath redeemed us from the curse of the law, being made a curse for us: for it is written Cursed *is* every one that hangeth on a tree: [14] That the blessing of Abraham might come on the Gentiles through Jesus Christ; that we might receive the promise of the Spirit through faith. (Galatians 3:11-14)

The term "The just shall live by faith" is found in four places in the Bible (Habakkuk 2:4; Romans 1:17; here in Galatians 3:11; and in Hebrews 10:38). It is a statement to the effect that it is faith that actually saved people whether under Law in the Old Testament, under grace today, or in the coming kingdom under the New Covenant. Under the Law, people performed the requirements of the Law but understood that it was their faith in what God said that actually saved and not the performance of the works of the Law. The redeeming work that Jesus accomplished on the cross removed the curse of the Law for us. Paul is pointing out here that the cross removed the curse of the conditional covenant of the Law that was added to the unconditional covenant that God made with Abraham 430 years earlier.

> [15] Brethren, I speak after the manner of men; though *it be* but a man's covenant, yet *if it be* confirmed, no man disannulleth, or addeth thereto. (Galatians 3:15)

Even in contracts between men, a contractual agreement is unalterable once it is made and agreed upon by both parties.

> [16] Now to Abraham and his seed were the promises made. He saith not, And to seeds, as of many; but as of one, And to thy seed, which is Christ. [17] And this I say, *that* the covenant, that was confirmed before of God in Christ, the law, which was four hundred and thirty years after, cannot disannul, that it should make the promise of none effect. [18] For if the inheritance *be* of the law, *it is* no more of promise: but God gave *it* to Abraham by promise. (Galatians 3:16-18)

God made an agreement (an unconditional covenant) with Abraham and Abraham's seed. That unconditional covenant is found in Genesis 13:15 and in Genesis Chapter 15. It is what we call the Abrahamic Covenant. Here the apostle tells us that it is not with the seeds (plural) but with Abraham's seed (singular). That seed is Christ. The blessing of that covenant will go to the multiplied seed of Abraham but only to those of his multiplied seed who will find the fulfillment of the promise in Christ. The covenant of the Law which came 430 years later cannot nullify the unconditional covenant that God made with Abraham. The inheritance in view here is eternal life. We understand that the promise is resurrection life in the land because God promised him and his seed the land of Canaan as an everlasting possession (Genesis 15:8). However, God also told him that he would die and be buried before getting it (Genesis 15:15). We therefore understand that the basic provision of the Abrahamic Covenant is eternal life that involves resurrection life in which he will inherit that land.

> [19] Wherefore then *serveth* the law? It was added because of transgressions, till the seed should come to whom

the promise was made; *and it was* ordained by angels in the hand of a mediator. [20] Now a mediator is not *a mediator* of one, but God is one. [21] Is the law then against the promises of God? God forbid: for if there had been a law given which could have given life, verily righteousness should have been by the law. (Galatians 3:19-21)

Why then did God give the Law? He added it because of Israel's transgression – her sin. Israel had to learn that they were as much in need of redemption as were the Gentiles. Therefore, God gave them the Law as a means of conviction. Performance of the Law could not save them but it served to point them to the blood sacrifice that did cover sin until the real sacrifice that got the job of redemption done was made by Christ.

[22] But the scripture hath concluded all under sin, that the promise by faith of Jesus Christ might be given to them that believe. [23] But before faith came, we were kept under the law, shut up unto the faith which should afterwards be revealed. [24] Wherefore the law was our schoolmaster *to bring us* unto Christ, that we might be justified by faith. [25] But after that faith is come, we are no longer under a schoolmaster. [26] For ye are all the children of God by faith in Christ Jesus. [27] For as many of you as have been baptized into Christ have put on Christ. (Galatians 3:22-27)

The scripture (represented by the Law) concluded all under sin that the promise of eternal life might be available to all by the faithfulness of Christ to accomplish redemption by His work of the cross. From the time of the giving of the Law until the revelation of the mystery of the gospel given through Paul, the human race was under the Law. The Law was then a school master to instruct people of their need of a redeemer. The faithfulness of Jesus on the cross has now opened up the way for us to be children of God. When we trust Jesus Christ and His work of redemption, the Holy Spirit baptizes us (living in this dispensation of grace) into an eternal spiritual relationship with Him to make us children of God (Gal. 3:27) – a baptism that has nothing to do with water. The dispensation of grace took us members of the body of Christ out from under law and put us under grace.

For Israel under the New Covenant, the Law will be put in their minds and written in their hearts (Jeremiah 31:31-34). What the Book of Hebrews is going to do is take Israel from the Old Covenant into the New Covenant that God will make with that nation. Under that New Covenant, God will put His laws into their minds, and write them in their hearts. (Heb. 8:10) Associated with this change in the Law there will be a change in the priesthood for Israel. This change involves Jesus Christ being a priest forever after the order of Melchisedec (Hebrews 5:6). The Book of Hebrews is as foundational to the gospel of the circumcision as the Book of Romans is to the gospel of the uncircumcision. Specifically, just as Romans presents the merits of Calvary in the context of our program today in the dispensation of grace, the Book of Hebrews does so for Israel in their kingdom program. The books of Hebrews through the Revelation will be the portion of scripture that will be preached by the two witnesses of Revelation 13:3 and by the 144,000 Jewish preachers in the Tribulation period.

- Paul says "For there is no difference between the Jew and the Greek..." (Rom 10:12) However, before Paul is sent to the world with the dispensation of grace (i.e., with the revelation of the mystery), there was a God-ordained difference between the Jew and the Gentile.
- Paul asks, "Is he the God of the Jews only?" (Rom 3:29) Before the dispensation of grace, He was the God of the Jews only (John 4:22).

Regarding the Law, Hebrews says that "The priesthood being changed, there is of necessity a change of the law..." (Heb 7:12) The New Covenant (which Hebrews presents to Israel) will encompass the Old Covenant in that God will put the law in their minds and write it in their hearts (Heb. 8:10 cf. Jer. 31:31-32). Paul tells us that God took the law out of the way to bring in the dispensation of grace (Col. 2:14) and that we are not under law but under grace (Rom. 6:14; Gal. 2:20 & 21). The Book of Hebrews says that God will replace the Old Covenant (the law) with the New Covenant. A review of the following verses will give the reader the flavor of the book of Hebrews regarding the relationship of the Law of Moses and the New Covenant that Hebrews present to Israel.

- Hebrews 7:19 "...the law made nothing perfect but the bringing in of a better hope did..."
- Hebrews 8:7 "For if the first covenant had been faultless, then should no place have been sought for the second."
- Hebrews 8:10-12 God would do for Israel (i.e. enable them to keep the law) what Israel could not do for herself.
- Hebrews 10:1 "...for the law ...can never ... make the comers thereunto perfect..."
- Hebrews 10:9 "...He taketh away the first that he may establish the second."
- Hebrews 10:16, 17 "...I will put my laws into their hearts, and in their minds will I write them; And their sins and iniquities will I remember no more."
- Hebrews 10:19 "Having therefore...boldness to enter into the holiest ... By a new and living way..."
- Hebrews 10:22 "Let us draw near... having our hearts sprinkled from an evil conscience, and our bodies washed with pure water..."

The message of the book of Hebrews regarding the work of Christ on the Cross is consistent with the Pauline epistles. However, there are aspects of Hebrews regarding the hope and the means of appropriating salvation that are inconsistent with the message in the Pauline epistles. The writer uses the all-inclusive "us" and "we" to tie himself and his hearers into the gospel that "...at first began to be spoken by the Lord ..." (Heb. 2:3). But during His earthly ministry, Jesus Christ was a minister of the Circumcision (Rom. 15:8; Matt. 10:15; 15:24). The Circumcision had a gospel that was separate and distinct from the gospel that belonged to the Uncircumcision. Paul was committed with the gospel of the Uncircumcision (Gal. 2:6-9). With that in mind, notice the "us" and the "we" in Hebrews: (Heb. 1:2, 2:3, 3:6, 4:1-2, 4:14, 6:3, 7:26, 8:1, 9:24, 13:13-14). The "us" of Hebrews 1:1 is Israel (Psa. 147:19-20, Rom. 2:14, Rom. 2:17, Rom. 3:2).

The Hebrew church epistles (Hebrews through Revelation) in general deal with:

- The Hebrew people reigning on Earth as a kingdom of priests.
- Israel being given instructions on how to get through the Tribulation.
- Israel needing faithfulness in their stand for the faith.
- How to hold forth the truth in a world of deception.
- How to identify false teachers.
- How to identify truth.
- First Peter says "the end of all things is at hand" (1Peter 4:7) – that is to say, the kingdom is at hand. Second Peter tells them that there is a delay before the kingdom will come (2Peter 3:15) and that you have to go to Paul's writings to understand why the delay happened.
- There is a sure hope that will keep you going.
- James is concerned with works necessary to get into the kingdom (James 2:17-22). The issue for them is faith that produces works (Matt. 25:37).
- The Book of Hebrews says "let us go on to perfection." That is to take the truth of what happened on Calvary and introduce it to the believing remnant of Israel. Jesus Christ is the High Priest of Israel. He

did not offer sacrifices as the Old Covenant priest did. He offered Himself as a once for all time sacrifice. Therefore, Israel was to leave the Old Covenant and its priesthood and go on to the New Covenant and to go on to a priest after the order of Melchisedec – that priest being our Lord Jesus Christ.

Hebrews speaks of going on to perfection. That means that the Hebrew people did not have perfection in the information presented in Matthew, Mark, Luke, and John or in that portion of the Book of Acts in which the kingdom was being offered to Israel. The Hebrew church epistles will take them on to perfection in their understanding of their program – especially in regard to the atonement in the shed blood of Christ.

Hebrews 6:1 "Leaving the principles of the doctrine of Christ, let us go on to perfection..."
Hebrews 7:11 "If therefore perfection were by the Levitical priesthood..."

Hebrews also speaks of going on to a better priesthood. The Pauline epistles say nothing about priesthood. That is because our relationship to God through Christ is based not on any Covenant that God made with anyone but on the information presented in the preaching of Jesus Christ according to the revelation of the mystery. Israel however has a relationship as a nation based on covenants that requires the office of a high priest. The Book of Hebrews takes Israel on:

- To the priesthood after the order of Melchisedec.
- To the New Covenant.
- To the Cross.
    - In Matthew, Mark, Luke, and John they did not understand the cross (Luke 9:15, 18:34, Matt. 16:3).
    - In early Acts, Peter still did not know about what was actually accomplished there on the cross except that it was prophesied (Acts 2:38). If Peter knew what was accomplished on the cross as the price of redemption, he did not teach it in any of his messages in the first chapters of the book of Acts.
    - Peter apparently learned about what was really accomplished on the cross from Paul (Note: Acts 15:11 "We shall be saved even as they..."). Note the table below on the two-fold aspect of Paul's ministry.

There is much debate about who wrote Hebrews. We know that God actually wrote it but the question is, "Who is the human author?" The author did not identify himself but it is clear that those who received it knew the author personally (Heb. 13:18-25). Probably a more important question is not who wrote the book but who did not write it. For those of us who understand the Word rightly divided, believing Paul wrote Hebrews is a problem in that the book is about Israel and their hope of a kingdom on Earth (Rev. 5:10), while the hope for the church the body of Christ (of which Paul in the first member -- 1Tim. 1:15) is a heavenly kingdom (2Tim. 4:18; 2Cor. 5:1, 21).

The Pauline revelation has two components to it. The first is related to what Paul refers to as "...the gospel of God (which he had promised afore by his prophets in the Holy Scriptures – Rom. 1:2) concerning his Son Jesus Christ..." This would take us back to Genesis 3:15 where the seed of the woman is first mentioned. The final piece of information revealed by Jesus Christ through Paul has to do with how the seed of the woman was going to defeat Satan. That information is presented in Romans Chapter Three. It is apparent that the writer of Hebrews got his information about what was accomplished on the cross from Paul. It is in the Pauline Epistles that we first encounter the preaching of the cross as "Good News." This component of the Pauline revelation relates to both Israel and the Body of Christ. It is the blood that Jesus Christ shed on Calvary that gives redemption to both Israel and the Body of Christ.

The second component of the Pauline revelation has to do with the preaching of Jesus Christ according to the revelation of the mystery. This has nothing to do with Israel or with what the prophets of the Old Testament had talked about regarding a kingdom to be set up on this earth through the nation of Israel. The preaching of Jesus Christ according to the revelation of the mystery pertains only to the Church which is Christ's body with its heavenly hope and destiny.

Paul was sent to bear Christ's name before the Gentiles, and kings, and the children of Israel (Act 9:15). There is a two fold aspect to his ministry.

Table 1 The Two fold Ministry of the Apostle Paul

	Rom 1:1-4	Rom 3:24-26	Rom 16:25-26
A ministry to both Israel and the Gentiles (Act 9:15, Eph. 1:9)	Paul...called to be an apostle, separated unto the gospel of God [Gen 3:15] (which he had promised afore by his prophets in the holy scriptures,) concerning his Son Jesus Christ...	Being justified freely by his grace through the redemption that is in Christ Jesus: whom God hath set forth to be a propitiation through faith in his blood to declare his righteousness for the remission of sins that are past through the forbearance of God...	Now to him that is of power to stablish you according to my gospel...
A ministry that was uniquely to the Gentiles (Rom. 11:25, 16:25, 1Cor. 2:7, 4:1, 15:51, Eph. 3:3-9, 5:32, Col. 1:26-27, 4:3, 2Thess. 2:7, 1Tim. 3:9, 16)			And the preaching of Jesus Christ according to the revelation of the mystery, which was kept secret since the world began, but now is made manifest and by the scriptures of the prophets [New Testament prophets] (1Cor. 14:37, Acts 15:32, Rom. 12:6)] according to the commandment of the everlasting God, made known to all nations for the obedience of faith.

Five Warnings in the Book of Hebrews

If there be a defined structure to the Book of Hebrews, it would be the five warnings that we find in the book. There are five warnings to the Hebrew people regarding things they can loose if they do not pay heed to the doctrine of this book. The warnings can be summarized as follows:

- The 1st Warning is in Hebrews 2:1-4 – Don't let the Words of the Son slip.
- The 2nd is in Hebrews 3:17 – 4:13 – Don't have an evil heart of unbelief as did Israel in the wilderness.
- The 3rd warning is in Hebrews 5:11- 6:20 – Don't be dull of hearing but be mature in your understanding.
- The 4th is in Hebrews 10:26-31 – Don't go back to the Old Testament sacrifices but go on the Christ and His all sufficient sacrifice.
- The 5th is in Hebrews 12:25-29 – Don't refuse Him who now (and will again in the future) speaks from Heaven.

Structural Analysis

The next page presents a structural analysis of Chapter 1 of the Book of Hebrews. It is presented for illustration purposes to show the student how such an analysis is done. The purpose for such an analysis is to lay out the main point of a passage of scripture across the page to identify the main point of the passage. The main point contains the entirety of the concept or idea and has two parts: the subject (or theme) and the predicate (or the thesis). The subject answers the question "What is the passage talking about?" The predicate answers the question "What is the passage saying about what it is talking about?" Subordinate clauses are then moved out of the main clause and are placed either above the line of the main clause or below the line based on whether they come before or after the main point in the passage.

The benefit of such an exercise is to give the student a clear view to gain understanding of the main point. After a structural analysis is made, the student can search deeper into the meaning of the Bible concept present by the passage by use of a cross reference such as the *Treasury of Scripture Knowledge*.

Structural Layout of Hebrews 1:1-14 (KJV)

who at sundry times ... spake unto the fathers ...
and in divers manners...   by the prophets,
in time past
       in these last days
[1] God,... [2] Hath ... spoken unto us by *his* Son, ...
[His Son] whom he hath appointed heir of all things, ...
    by whom also he made the worlds;
     [3] Who being the brightness of *his* glory, ...
    and the express image of his person, ...
    and upholding all things by the word of his power, ...
    when he had ... sat down on the right hand of the Majesty on high;
         by himself purged our sins,
    [4] Being made so much better than the angels, ...
      as he hath by inheritance obtained a more excellent name than they.

[5] For unto which of the angels said he at any time, ...
      Thou art my Son, this day have I begotten thee? ...
      And again, I will be to him a Father, ...
        and he shall be to me a Son?
           when he bringeth in the firstbegotten into the world
      [6] And again, ..., he saith, And let all the angels of God worship him. [7] And of the angels he saith, Who maketh his angels spirits,...
          and his ministers a flame of fire.

       unto the Son
[8] But ... *he saith*, Thy throne, O God, *is* for ever and ever:...
         a sceptre of righteousness *is* the sceptre of thy kingdom.
        [9] Thou hast loved righteousness, ...
          and hated iniquity; ...
         even thy God
       therefore God, ..., hath anointed thee with the oil of gladness above thy fellows.
        Lord,
[10] And, Thou,... in the beginning hast laid the foundation of the earth; ...
         and the heavens are the works of thine hands:
      [11] They shall perish; ...
        but thou remainest; ...
     and they all shall wax old as doth a garment; [12] And as a vesture shalt thou fold them up, ...
     and they shall be changed: ...
        but thou art the same, ...
        and thy years shall not fail.
[13] But to which of the angels said he at any time, Sit on my right hand, ...
          until I make thine enemies thy footstool?
[14] Are they not all ministering spirits, ...
sent forth to minister for them who shall be heirs of salvation?

Study Guide Questions on the Introduction

1. On which of the offices that the Lord Jesus Christ holds does the Book of Hebrews focus?
2. List the steps in the three step process by which God appeals to Israel to trust in Jesus as Messiah.
3. Through whom did the Father appeal to Israel and when did that occur in the New Testament?
4. Where in Matthew's gospel do we see the Son's appeal to Israel?
5. What was the Holy Spirit tying to accomplish with Israel through Peter's message in Acts 3: 12-23?
6. How long, according to Acts 2:22-36, was Jesus to sit at the Father's right hand?
7. What should have happened according to the prophetic clock when Israel blasphemed the Holy Ghost by stoning Stephen to death? What actually did happen?
8. What is the focal point of the Hebrew church epistles (Hebrews through the Revelation)?

CHAPTER 1
THE SON SPEAKS TO ISRAEL

Chapter 1 presents our Lord Jesus Christ as the Son of God the Father (the Son of God). In 2:1 through 4:12, He is presented as the Son of Man. Then in 4:13 through Chapter 10, He is presented as the High Priest. The Book of Hebrews is about the priesthood of Jesus Christ. Israel had learned about the priesthood of the Law under the Old Covenant. There was a tribe of Israel that was designated as the priestly tribe under the Old Covenant. That tribe represented Israel before God. God was teaching the nation that ultimately they would be a kingdom of priests to represent the Gentiles before God. However, before that could be accomplished, Israel would have to be redeemed by the blood of the New Covenant. The New Covenant will have a different priesthood than the Old Covenant did. We will be learning about that New Covenant and new priesthood as we study this amazing book of Hebrews.

Hebrews Chapter 1

> **Hebrews 1:1-4** "God, who at sundry times and in divers manners spake in time past unto the fathers by the prophets, ² Hath in these last days spoken unto us by *his* Son, whom he hath appointed heir of all things, by whom also he made the worlds; ³ Who being the brightness of *his* glory, and the express image of his person, and upholding all things by the word of his power, when he had by himself purged our sins, sat down on the right hand of the Majesty on high; ⁴ Being made so much better than the angels, as he hath by inheritance obtained a more excellent name than they."

According to Verse 1, God had in time past spoken unto the fathers of Israel by the prophets but has in the last days spoken unto us [the Hebrew people] by His Son. This key book of the Bible is about the Hebrew people in relation to Jesus Christ the Son of God. God spoke through the prophets in the past to tell of the coming of Jesus Christ the Son, but now the Son has spoken to them. The days in which the Son speaks are the last days because His word is the last word to Israel. That is to say that He (the Son) will consummate God's purpose for the nation. Israel's program centers in the Son and in the kingdom that God will establish on earth through Him.

In the book of Acts (Acts 10:28, 15:7-12, 18:24-28), we see that there is an interruption in Israel's program. In Romans Chapters 9, 10, and 11 we see the apostle of the Gentiles explain that interruption. In fact, in 2Peter 3:3-16, we see Peter directing his readers to Paul's epistles to explain the interruption in Israel's program. Note particularly verses 15 and 16:

¹⁵ And account *that* the longsuffering of our Lord *is* salvation; even as our beloved brother Paul also according to the wisdom given unto him hath written unto you; ¹⁶ As also in all *his* epistles, speaking in them of these things; in which are some things hard to be understood, which they that are unlearned and unstable wrest, as *they do* also the other scriptures, unto their own destruction.   (2Peter 3:15-16)

The Book of Hebrews is about Israel's program again being advanced. Their program will not resume until after the preaching of Jesus Christ according to the revelation of the Mystery is completed. That will not happen until the Dispensation of Grace comes to a close with the church which is His Body being caught up to meet the Lord in the air (the unseen realm of heaven where it will spend eternity – 2Cor. 5:1). This catching away is the event that we call the rapture. It precedes the start of the Seventieth week of Daniel Chapter 9. God has an eternal purpose for the heavenly places that He is administering today during the Dispensation of Grace by the calling out of the Gentile church – the church which is His body. The book of Hebrews will then present to Israel the blood atonement much like how the Book of Romans presented it to us today in the dispensation of grace. It, along with the rest of the circumcision epistles of Hebrews through Revelation, presents the doctrine that will take Israel through the coming Tribulation Period that follows the rapture and into the kingdom. The doctrine of Hebrews transitions Israel from the Old Testament Law to the New Covenant established in the redemption through the blood of Christ as Israel's High Priest.

We get a glimpse of what Israel expected of the Messiah by passages such as John 4:25 where the woman at the well says: "25 ... I know that Messias cometh, which is called Christ: when he is come, he will tell us all things." Note the Lord's own words on the matter in John 15:15... "15 Henceforth I call you not servants; for the servant knoweth not what his lord doeth: but I have called you friends; for all things that I have heard of my Father I have made known unto you."

In Acts we see the believing remnant of Israel zealous of the Law (Acts 21:20). They are doing what they were taught to do by our Lord in Matthew 23:1-4. To understand the transition that will happen in Israel as the nation moves from the Old Covenant of the Law to the New Covenant (which Hebrews will present to the nation) we need to follow the Lord's instruction to the apostles who will eventually bring the nation into her New Covenant. We go first to the commission that the Lord gives to the twelve apostles in Matthew 28:20:

> "16 Then the eleven disciples went away into Galilee, into a mountain where Jesus had appointed them. 17 And when they saw him, they worshipped him: but some doubted. 18 And Jesus came and spake unto them, saying, All power is given unto me in heaven and in earth. 19 Go ye therefore, and teach all nations, baptizing them in the name of the Father, and of the Son, and of the Holy Ghost: 20 Teaching them to observe all things whatsoever I have commanded you: and, lo, I am with you alway, *even* unto the end of the world. Amen."   (Matthew 28:16-20)

These are the closing words of Matthew's gospel. Note some important points here: Because of His victory over death and sin, all power is given to Him in heaven and in earth. The full impact of these words will be seen only after more information about the cross is revealed in the Pauline epistles. For now however, we note that they were "...to observe all things whatsoever I have commanded you..." Now before reading more into this than what is here, let's go back to Matthew 23: 1-5 to note some things that the Lord commanded them

> "1 Then spake Jesus to the multitude, and to his disciples, 2 Saying, The scribes and the Pharisees sit in Moses' seat: 3 All therefore whatsoever they bid you observe, *that* observe and do; but do not ye after their works: for they say, and do not."   (Matthew 23:1-3)

In Matthew 28, Jesus is telling Israel through the twelve apostles to continue to maintain the precepts of the Law of Moses. Note also from Matthew 28:20 that they were to go into all the world baptizing them in the name of the Trinity – "... in the name [singular] of the Father, and of the Son, and of the Holy Ghost." Water baptism was the rite whereby the Levites were inducted into the priesthood. (Exodus 29:4; 40:12) Water baptism was also a cleansing rite that God instituted in Numbers 19:1-8. It is not called baptism in the Old Testament scriptures because the word baptism is not a translation but is rather a transliteration of the Greek word in which the New Testament scriptures were written. The New Testament "Baptism" is equivalent to the Old Testament "Washings." It is a cleansing rite involving water. Numbers 19:9 tells us what the rite does: "9 And a man *that is* clean shall gather up the ashes of the heifer, and lay *them* up without the camp in a clean place, and it shall be kept for the congregation of the children of Israel for a water of separation: it *is* a purification for sin." Numbers 19:9 (KJV)

Water Baptism and the Law of Moses were still required institutions in God's program with Israel as they go into

Pentecost in the Book of Acts. This is the "...baptism of repentance for the remission of sins" that John preached to Israel (Mark 1:4; Luke 3:3). In Matthew 3:4 we see John puzzled by the Lord coming to him to be baptized. John did not understand it yet but there were two reasons for this action by our Lord – both of which will be manifest in the Book of Hebrews. That baptism was first of all His (Christ's) induction into the priesthood. Secondly, it was a fulfillment of Isaiah 53:8-11 whereby He was identified with the transgressors.

"⁸ He was taken from prison and from judgment: and who shall declare his generation? for he was cut off out of the land of the living: for the transgression of my people was he stricken. ⁹ And he made his grave with the wicked, and with the rich in his death; because he had done no violence, neither *was any* deceit in his mouth. ¹⁰ Yet it pleased the LORD to bruise him; he hath put *him* to grief: when thou shalt make his soul an offering for sin, he shall see *his* seed, he shall prolong *his* days, and the pleasure of the LORD shall prosper in his hand. ¹¹ He shall see of the travail of his soul, *and* shall be satisfied: by his knowledge shall my righteous servant justify many; for he shall bear their iniquities." (Isaiah 53:8-11)

For Israelites, water baptism identified the sinner with their Messiah and the Messiah with the transgressors. It was the means whereby the Messiah could bear their iniquities and the Father could thereby "Justify many." We today who live in the dispensation of grace have a baptism that transfers our sin and guilt to the Savior and His righteousness to us but that baptism has nothing to do with water (1Cor. 12:12 - 13; 2Cor. 5:21). So too, there is a difference in how the Law is applied in Israel's New Covenant and how it operates for us members of the Body of Christ today. For us, God took the law out of the way "...nailing it to his cross" (Col. 2:14). However, for Israel under the New Covenant, God is going to "put my laws into their mind and write them in their hearts..." (Heb. 8:10). The nation will, when the book of Hebrews is preached during the Tribulation Period, have to leave the Old Covenant and go on to the New Covenant. But that New Covenant will encompass the Old Testament Law in such a way that Israel will be empowered by the New Covenant to keep the Law.

The term "these last days" in Hebrews 1:2 is significant. We find the term first used in Genesis 49:1 "¹ And Jacob called unto his sons, and said, Gather yourselves together, that I may tell you *that* which shall befall you in the last days." The term is a reference to the salvation and blessings to Israel. The term "the last day" is a reference to resurrection and judgment (2 Tim. 3:1). The term "the latter times" (1Tim. 4:1), "the latter days," and "the latter years" (Ezek. 38:8) are all referring to the Tribulation Period. Two key passages on the last days are Isaiah 2:2-4 and Micah 4:1-3. It should be noted that the writer of Hebrews considered himself to be in the last days.

"² And it shall come to pass in the last days, *that* the mountain of the LORD'S house shall be established in the top of the mountains, and shall be exalted above the hills; and all nations shall flow unto it. ³ And many people shall go and say, Come ye, and let us go up to the mountain of the LORD, to the house of the God of Jacob; and he will teach us of his ways, and we will walk in his paths: for out of Zion shall go forth the law, and the word of the LORD from Jerusalem. ⁴ And he shall judge among the nations, and shall rebuke many people: and they shall beat their swords into plowshares, and their spears into pruninghooks: nation shall not lift up sword against nation, neither shall they learn war any more." (Isaiah 2:2-4)

" But in the last days it shall come to pass, *that* the mountain of the house of the LORD shall be established in the top of the mountains, and it shall be exalted above the hills; and people shall flow unto it. ² And many nations shall come, and say, Come, and let us go up to the mountain of the LORD, and to the house of the God of Jacob; and he will teach us of his ways, and we will walk in his paths: for the law shall go forth of Zion, and the word of the LORD from Jerusalem. ³ And he shall judge among many people, and rebuke strong nations afar off; and they shall beat their swords into plowshares, and their spears into pruninghooks: nation shall not lift up a sword against nation, neither shall they learn war any more." (Micah 4:1-3)

Hebrews 1:2 and following present the Son in relation to the Father:
- The Father spoke through the Son.
- The Father made the Son heir of all things (cf. John 1:1-4, 1Cor. 8:6, Eph. 3:9, Col. 1:16-17, Isa. 45: 12, et al).
- The Father effected creation through the Son.
- The Son is the brightness of the Father's glory (Eph. 1:17, Matt. 25: 31).
- The Son is the express image of the Father's person (John 14: 8-9, Col. 1:15).
- The Son holds all things by the word of His power.
- The Son purged Israel's sins and then sat down at the Father's right hand.

The Son has inherited a more excellent name than the angels.

We see therefore that, after the Dispensation of Grace closes, Israel will go on in their program from the Old Covenant unto the New Covenant. The doctrine of Hebrews will do that for them (Heb. 8:13, 13:10).

The Lord during His earthly ministry was sent only to the house of Israel (Matt. 10:5; 15:24) to confirm the promises that God had made to the nation (Rom. 15:8). Access to God belongs naturally to Israel (Rom. 10: 18-22). The Gentiles in this present dispensation of grace are temporarily grafted into that place of access to God contrary to nature (Rom. 11:24). However, the covenant is with Israel and the gifts and callings of God are without repentance (Rom. 11:29). In the Book of Acts and in the circumcision epistles, we find Israel scattered (Acts 2:5, 8:1; James 1:1; 1Peter 1:1, etc.). One day in the future, Israel again will be scattered (Luke 21: 20-24). Though many in Israel believed during the period of Acts (Acts 4:8, 1Peter 1:18), the nation at large was in unbelief (Rom. 10:3).

Hebrews 1:3 "...When he had by himself purged our sins, sat down on the right hand of the Majesty on high..." speaks of Christ being seated at the right hand of the Father. This is a sign that He is appointed heir of all things. Christ is the express image of the Father's person and is the Creator and Redeemer. The Lord Jesus Christ came to be a Son to the Father to show Israel how to live as a son. When the Lord calls Israel out of Egypt He says of the nation "Israel is my son, even my first born." (Ex. 4:22). The Lord was not called the Son until He entered into humanity. Before that, He was the eternal Word (John 1:1-4, 14) from eternity past. However, He became the "firstbegotten" (Heb. 1:6) when He entered into humanity.

Israel as a nation was to be a kingdom of priests (Exodus 19:6) and a royal priesthood (1Peter 2:9). The term "firstbegotten" implies that there will be others who are also begotten in a similar manner. 1Peter 1:3 speaks of this being "begotten again unto a lively hope by the resurrection of Jesus Christ from the dead..." Christ entered humanity to show Israel how to be sons of God and a kingdom of priests. When the Lord Jesus Christ enters the world, the Father makes it clear that He as the representative man is superior to the angels. To do this He has the angels worship the Son. It will eventually be that man (mankind) will find the fulfillment of what God created man to be in the person of the Son. Though man was created lower than the angels (Heb. 2:7) at the original creation, he (man) will one day be the eternal custodian of God's creation (Heb. 2:5). Jesus Christ is the "only begotten Son" as to His physical birth (John 3:16). He is the first begotten relative to His resurrection (Heb. 1:6; Rev. 1:5). He is the first in a line of others who will be raised from the dead. In Romans 8:29 He is the "firstborn among many brethren." In Colossians 1:18, He is the "firstborn from the dead." In Hebrews 12:23 the entire body of believers (i.e. the believers of Israel) is referred to as the "church of the firstborn."

The "when" of verse 3 is important! When was He made so much better than the angels and when did He (by inheritance) obtain a more excellent name than they? It was when He had by Himself purged Israel's sins and sat down on the right hand of the Majesty on high.

In verse 4 Christ was "...made so much better than the angels, as he hath by inheritance obtained a more excellent name than they." He has a more excellent name than the angels in that He inherited it as the Son.

> **Hebrews 1:5-8** "For unto which of the angels said he at any time, Thou art my Son, this day have I begotten thee? And again, I will be to him a Father, and he shall be to me a Son? ⁶ And again, when he bringeth in the firstbegotten into the world, he saith, And let all the angels of God worship him. ⁷ And of the angels he saith, Who maketh his angels spirits, and his ministers a flame of fire. ⁸ But unto the Son *he saith*, Thy throne, O God, *is* for ever and ever: a sceptre of righteousness *is* the sceptre of thy kingdom."

Verse 5 makes reference to angels. We ask ourselves, "Why the reference to angels here in Hebrews?" In answer to that we note that angels had a significant role that they played in Israel's history and will again in the future. Angels are ministering spirits who minister salvation to Israel. Our relationship to angels today in the Dispensation of Grace is entirely different than was the relationship of angels to men in Israel's program. Today angels are learning about the wisdom of God by observing the grace of God making a positive impact in our lives as we walk by faith in the grace that is ours in Christ (Eph. 3:10). In Israel's program, they were actively involved in delivering Israel from her enemies. The writer of Hebrews here now in this epistle directs Israel's attention away from angels to the Son as the deliverer.

The law was "...ordained by angels in the hands of a mediator." (Gal. 3:19). It was "spoken by angels..." (Heb. 2:2). Angels were apparently involved in the establishing of the Law and in fact it may have been written by angels. Paul in Colossians 2:18 speaks of the Old Covenant as the "worshipping of angels." It was the worshipping of servitude of the law – the kind of servitude that angels would do. However, Israel's blessings were not going to come to Israel through Moses and the Law, but through Christ and the New Covenant. Therefore, Hebrews directs these Israelites away from the focus on angels to a focus on Christ.

Verse 5 quotes the second Psalm "Thou art my Son, this day have I begotten thee." Interestingly though, the scripture applies this not just to His birth (or to His conception) but to His resurrection (Acts 13:33). He was begotten of God in the virgin's womb to become a man. However, he was begotten at his resurrection to become a high priest forever after the order of Melchisedec (more on this later as we study Hebrews 5:9 and 8:1). Note the time element in Hebrews 1:3, "...when he had by himself purged our sins, sat down at the right hand of the Majesty on high..." This again indicates that the begetting happened at the resurrection. We start to understand that the Lord entered into a different kind of ministry at this resurrection than He had while on earth.

Verse 6 is a quote from Psalm 97:7. "⁷ Confounded be all they that serve graven images, that boast themselves of idols: worship him, all *ye* gods." Here angels are referred to as gods. Angels are called gods in this verse because they are powerful created beings created as free-moral-agents. Man is also a free moral agent but not as powerful as angels. Angels and men are free in that they are free to act. They are moral in that they know right from wrong. They are agents in that they are accorded opportunity to act independently of God if they so chose but they are and will be held responsible for their individual decisions. Eventually, all free moral agent (angelic or human) will one day give account to God for their actions.

In Verse 8 we see the Father referring to the Son as God "⁸ But unto the Son *he saith*, Thy throne, O God, *is* for ever and ever..." This is a statement on the deity of Jesus Christ. Jesus Christ is God from eternity past to eternity future.

In fact He is God from before time even began for He is the one who created the space, matter and time continuum that is the created universe.

- As God the Son, He rules over everything.
- As the Son of Abraham, He would rule over Israel.
- As the Son of Adam, He would rule over the world of men.
- As the Son of God, He would rule over God's entire universe.

Jesus is the only begotten Son relative to His physical birth. He is the first begotten from the dead relative to His resurrection. Paul refers to Him as the firstborn among many brethren (Rom. 8:29). Hebrews 12:23 refers to the general assembly of believers as the church of the firstborn. In Revelation 1:5, He is referred to as the first begotten from the dead. His work of redemption meant that He was the first to arise in resurrection life with a whole line of others to follow as a result of His redeeming work on Calvary.

> **Hebrews 1:9** – 12 "Thou hast loved righteousness, and hated iniquity; therefore God, *even* thy God, hath anointed thee with the oil of gladness above thy fellows. [10] And, Thou, Lord, in the beginning hast laid the foundation of the earth; and the heavens are the works of thine hands: [11] They shall perish; but thou remainest; and they all shall wax old as doth a garment; [12] And as a vesture shalt thou fold them up, and they shall be changed: but thou art the same, and thy years shall not fail."

In Verses 9 to 12, the Lord Jesus is likened to a man who dressed Himself in His creation. The whole universe is like a garment that He put on and that He will one day take off and put on another garment. He changes His garments but He himself never changes. His creation will change but the Creator will not change.

> **Hebrews 1:13** "But to which of the angels said he at any time, Sit on my right hand, until I make thine enemies thy footstool? [14] Are they not all ministering spirits, sent forth to minister for them who shall be heirs of salvation?"

Verse 13 is a quote from Psalm 110:1. This is also quoted in Acts 2:34 – 36. Every thing in His creation belongs to Him but His creation has been temporarily usurped and taken from Him. It is all His by right of creation and it will again be His by right of redemption. However, He is seated at the Father's right hand temporarily until it is time for Him to take back what is rightfully His. Peter quotes Psalm 110 in Acts 2, "[34] For David is not ascended into the heavens: but he saith himself, The LORD said unto my Lord, Sit thou on my right hand, [35] Until I make thy foes thy footstool. [36] Therefore let all the house of Israel know assuredly, that God hath made that same Jesus, whom ye have crucified, both Lord and Christ." (Acts 2:34-36). The Lord, when He ascended, sat down at the Father's right hand and would be there until it was time to make His enemies His footstool. In Acts Chapter 7, Stephen says, "[56] ... Behold, I see the heavens opened, and the Son of man standing on the right hand of God (Acts 7:56)." The fact that Stephen sees the Lord standing at the Father's right hand meant that it was time to make His enemies His footstool. That meant that the one year interruption in the prophetic timetable of Daniel 9:26 between the end of the 69th week and the beginning of the seventieth week (see Luke 13:8) was up. The Lord did indeed return to earth on schedule. However, He did not return to receive the Kingdom (Luke. 19:12) at that time as the Prophetic Program suggested He would. Rather, He returned to save Saul of Tarsus who was leading Israel's rejection of Christ. He saved Saul of Tarsus to then make him the one through whom He would reveal the Mystery Program. The great mystery that Jesus revealed through Paul is all about the Dispensation of Grace. The Dispensation of Grace in which we live is then another interruption in the Prophetic program. This second interruption will last until the present dispensation closes with the rapture of the church, the Body of Christ, to heaven. Then the Prophetic Program will pick up again beginning with the preaching of the Book of Hebrews by the 144,000 Jewish preachers in the Tribulation Period (Rev. 7:4).

Study Guides Questions on Chapter 1

1. The last words spoken by God to Israel were by whom?
2. What was it that interrupted God's program with Israel?
3. What event prophesied in Paul's epistles precedes the restart of Israel's prophetic program?
4. What did water baptism do for the believing Israelite?
5. To what time period does the term "the last days" in Hebrews 1:2 refer?
6. To who was Jesus Christ exclusively sent to by the Father during His earthly ministry?
7. What does the term "first begotten" in verse 6 imply regarding Jesus?
8. To what time frame does the word "when" in verse 3 apply?
9. How does Israel's relationship to angels in Hebrews differ from ours who live in the dispensation of grace?
10. When did the begetting of Verse 5 happen? What did that begetting accomplish?
11. Verse 6 refers to Jesus as the first begotten while John 3:18 and Hebrews 11:19 refer to Him as the only begotten. Explain the difference.
12. How do Verses 9-12 view creation relative to Jesus?

CHAPTER 2
DON'T LET THE WORDS OF THE SON SLIP

The First Warning

> **Hebrews 2:1-4** "Therefore we ought to give the more earnest heed to the things which we have heard, lest at any time we should let *them* slip. ² For if the word spoken by angels was stedfast, and every transgression and disobedience received a just recompence of reward; ³ How shall we escape, if we neglect so great salvation; which at the first began to be spoken by the Lord, and was confirmed unto us by them that heard *him*; ⁴ God also bearing *them* witness, both with signs and wonders, and with divers miracles, and gifts of the Holy Ghost, according to his own will?"

The First Warning in Hebrews -- Don't let the Words of the Son slip.

Verse 1 issues the first of a series of warnings in Hebrews. The warning here is: "Don't let the Words of the Son slip." It is easy to drift off of the course that is set for us and to drift into the world. (Matt. 16:9, Mark 8:18, 2Peter 2:12). The term "let them slip" is literally "to run from a leaking bucket." The things they are warned not to let slip away are in regard to the great salvation that verse 3 talks about. These are redemption truths which might slip away if the Hebrews don't give heed to the words that the Lord taught in Matthew, Mark, Luke, and John and by Peter at Pentecost. The salvation that is referred to here began to be spoken to them during the gospel era (during the Lord's public ministry) but these Hebrew people now need to go on in their understanding.

Verse 2 speaks of the word spoken by angels. This is a reference to the Old Covenant. Galatians 3:19 speaks of the Law as having been ordained by angels in the hands of a mediator (Gal 3:19). Angels were apparently involved in the writing of the Law while Moses was the one who was sent by God to mediate it. It might be that it was drafted in its entirety by angels. We see angels involved in Israel's program throughout the Old Testament. We see them in the Book of Daniel influencing the affairs of politics among men (Dan 4:17). In the Pauline epistles, we see that the Law has been taken out of the way for us (Col. 2:14). The Law could not produce the righteous standard that it demanded of man because it depended on our flesh. However, grace is all dependent upon the working of God through the word of His grace on the regenerated heart of the believer (Rom. 8:1-4). Grace therefore can and will produce within the believer today the standard of conduct that the Law demanded but could not produce (Rom. 5:20). Thereby, grace shows to the principalities and powers in heavenly places (Eph. 3:10) the manifold wisdom of God. What we will see in the Book of Hebrews is that God will write the Law in the hearts of the Hebrew people so that they will be able to keep it. This is the New Covenant that God will make with them (Jer. 31:33) when Israel's real Day of Atonement comes with the Lord's physical return to the nation to set up the kingdom (Acts 3:19).

Stephen in Acts 7:53 said that Israel received the Law by the disposition of angels. Verse 2 of this chapter says the Law was spoken by angels. Paul says that the Law was ordained by angels (Gal. 3:19). Angels apparently drafted the Law. However the Law (The Old Covenant) could not produce the righteousness that it demanded. Therefore, a New Covenant is needed. The Law while it was in effect was "steadfast." The great salvation referred to in verse 3 is the New Covenant which this book will introduce to the Hebrew people. The Hebrews are here warned that they shall not escape if they neglect it.

"Every transgression and disobedience received a just recompense of reward..." The disobedient of Israel were slain by the Law (Deut. 32:26-28). The Old Testament is full of illustrations of such punishment under the Law:

- Leviticus 24:14 - The boy that cursed was stoned.
- Numbers 11:23 - People died for lusting for meat instead of manna.
- Numbers 14:28 - Those who believed the ten spies and not the two men of faith (Caleb and Joshua) would die in the wilderness.
- Numbers 15:30-36 - Presumptuous sin resulted in being "Cut off" – put to death.
- Numbers 16:31-35 - The earth opened up to swallow those who followed Korah in the rebellion.
- Deuteronomy. 4:3-4 - Those that followed Baal-Peor died in the wilderness (cf. Josh. 22:17).
- Deuteronomy 17:2, 5, 17 Idolaters were to be stoned.

Those things listed here are an example to us not to lust after evil things (2Cor. 10:5-12). However, God deals with us who live under the dispensation of grace on the basis of grace and not law. Nevertheless we learn from those passages how God feels about sin.

Verse 3 speaks of a salvation which at the first began to be spoken by the Lord. We who live in the Dispensation of Grace have a salvation but our salvation was not a salvation which at the first began to be spoken by the Lord during His earthly ministry. The salvation that began to be spoken by the Lord was the salvation of Israel (the Hebrew people). Consider the words of Zacharias the father of John the Baptist regarding John the forerunner of Christ in Luke 1:68 - 80 " [68] Blessed *be* the Lord God of Israel; for he hath visited and redeemed his people, [69] And hath raised up an horn of salvation for us in the house of his servant David; [70] As he spake by the mouth of his holy prophets, which have been since the world began: [71] That we should be saved from our enemies, and from the hand of all that hate us; [72] To perform the mercy *promised* to our fathers, and to remember his holy covenant; [73] The oath which he sware to our father Abraham, [74] That he would grant unto us, that we being delivered out of the hand of our enemies might serve him without fear, [75] In holiness and righteousness before him, all the days of our life. [76] And thou, child, shalt be called the prophet of the Highest: for thou shalt go before the face of the Lord to prepare his ways; [77] To give knowledge of salvation unto his people by the remission of their sins, [78] Through the tender mercy of our God; whereby the dayspring from on high hath visited us, [79] To give light to them that sit in darkness and *in* the shadow of death, to guide our feet into the way of peace. [80] And the child grew, and waxed strong in spirit, and was in the deserts till the day of his shewing unto Israel."

It should be noted here that the salvation that at the first began to be spoken by the Lord is not the same salvation that we have today. The salvation of Israel is a salvation that will come to them in the Kingdom. So too, our salvation was not confirmed unto us by them that heard Him during His earthly ministry to Israel. Our salvation is based on the mystery that the Lord first revealed to us through the apostle Paul. Also, our salvation was not witnessed by signs and wonders as Israel's was at Pentecost (Mark 16:17).

The exodus of Israel out of Egypt (Ex. 12) is a type of the salvation of the Hebrews in Verse 3. Israel was delivered by blood when the death angel passed over the houses of Israel because of the Passover blood. Israel was delivered by power at the crossing of the Red Sea when Moses led the nation through the waters on dry land while the Egyptians who tried to follow were destroyed. In the Exodus, Egypt is a type of the world while Pharaoh is a type of Satan. The Book of Hebrews presents the antitype of the deliverance by blood while the Book of the Revelation presents the antitype of the deliverance by power.

Moses was the means of God delivering Israel during the Exodus. However, Moses is a type of another prophet. In the gospels there is a reference to "That Prophet" (John 1:21). Israel was to look for a prophet like unto Moses (Deut. 18:15-18). John the Baptist specifically said to those who came from Israel's leaders that he was not that prophet. That prophet like unto Moses was Christ who would deliver Israel from the world into the kingdom -- first by blood and then by power. John the Baptist would then have been Elijah had Israel accepted the offer of the Kingdom (Matt. 17:10-12). This would have put everything in place for a bona fide offer of the Kingdom to have been made in the Book of Acts. The first seven chapters of the book of Acts does indeed present to Israel a genuine offer of the kingdom. Had the nation repented of having crucified their Messiah, the Lord would have returned and set up the Kingdom.

Israel was born as a nation to be God's son. Moses was to tell Pharaoh as God's spokesman "...Israel is my son even my first born." (Ex 4:22). God's command was that Israel be separate from Egypt. God had Moses tell Pharaoh, "¹⁸ And they shall hearken to thy voice: and thou shalt come, thou and the elders of Israel, unto the king of Egypt, and ye shall say unto him, The LORD God of the Hebrews hath met with us: and now let us go, we beseech thee, three days' journey into the wilderness, that we may sacrifice to the LORD our God." (Exodus 3:18). God knew that Pharaoh would not let Israel go (Ex 3:19). Ultimately, the Egyptians would expel the Israelites (Ex 12:30-33) but He had an important lesson to teach them in making this request for a three day journey into the wilderness. Three is a number for God and also the number for perfection. Israel was to be completely separated from Egypt unto God in a resurrected life (new life separate from the world and from Satan). In Exodus, we see God telling Moses to tell Pharaoh to let Israel go three days' journey into the wilderness (Ex. 3:18). The concept was that there is to be a separation from the world (represented by Egypt) unto God (three days – three being the number for God and also the number for the resurrection). God knew that Pharaoh would not let Israel go (Ex. 3:19). As noted above, God also knew that Pharaoh will eventually send Israel out and then seek to destroy the nation. God would redeem Israel with blood (by means of the Passover in Egypt) and with power (at the crossing of the Red Sea).

Let's consider the three days' journey and the concept of separation from the world. Separation from the world and from Satan is a concept that is not hard to understand but it is difficult to achieve. The world and Satan are always looking for compromise. In Exodus Chapters 6 and 7 God sends three plagues which fall on Egypt and Israel alike. However, from Chapter 8 of Exodus on, there is a separation between Israel and Egypt (Ex 8:23) as far as the plagues was concerned. In chapter 8, Pharaoh was willing to let the children of Israel go but he fights the separation and is constantly trying for compromise that would not make the separation complete. Pharaoh's proposals were:
1. Don't go very far (Ex 8:28).
2. Only the men go and the children and cattle stay (Ex 10:11).
3. The children may go but the cattle stay (Ex 10:26-28).
Remember that Pharaoh was a type of Satan and Egypt a type of the world.

The "so great a salvation..." of Verse 3 is not only a salvation from hell and the lake of fire but also a salvation of the soul in physical deliverance to God (Isa. 12:2) into the Kingdom. The warning is to escape the wrath of the Lamb (Rev. 6:16 & 17). There is a similar warning to the world today in 1Thessalonians 5:3. No one who misses the rapture will escape the tribulation that follows. God will then "...send them strong delusion, that they should believe a lie. That they might be damned who believed not the truth, but had pleasure in unrighteousness." (2 Thess. 2:11-12). What a terrible time that will be. But the Tribulation Period is all about the Lord getting Israel saved (Rom. 11:26). In Luke 21:36, the Lord tells Israel how they can escape the wrath of that day. In Luke 19:9-10 the Lord says, "This day is salvation come to this house, [Zacchaeus' house] for as much as he also is a son of Abraham. For the Son of man is come to seek and to save that which was lost." (Speaking here of the lost of the house of Israel). We today are saved by grace apart from works (Eph. 2:8-10). However, Israel's salvation is different. Israel's salvation is by faith but it is by a faith that produces works (Matt. 5:20 and James 2:22).

Verse 4 speaks of the fact that God also bore witness to Israel with signs, wonders, miracles, and gifts of the Spirit. God not only had eyewitnesses but He also provided what we call "sign gifts". Therefore, in Israel's program, "These signs shall follow them that believe" (Mark 16:17). In Matthew 16:20 "...They went forth and preached everywhere, the Lord working with them, and confirming the word with signs following..." We see these signs used to great effect in the early part of the book of Acts (2:32-33, 3:15-16, 4:10, 14:3, 19:11-12, etc.). These signs were not for them that believe, but for them that believe not (1Cor. 14:22). At Pentecost, the signs were not for the benefit of the believing remnant of Israel but for the rest of the unbelieving nation. After He temporarily set the nation aside, the signs were evident among some Gentiles but it was again for a sign to the unbelieving nation (1Cor. 12:4-11 cf. Acts 18:7).

> **Hebrews 2:5-8** "For unto the angels hath he not put in subjection the world to come, whereof we speak. ⁶ But one in a certain place testified, saying, What is man, that thou art mindful of him? or the Son of man, that thou visitest him? ⁷ Thou madest him a little lower than the angels; thou crownedst him with glory and honour, and didst set him over the works of thy hands: ⁸ Thou hast put all things in subjection under his feet. For in that he put all in subjection under him, he left nothing *that is* not put under him. But now we see not yet all things put under him."

We see in verse 5 that the world to come is the subject of the book of Hebrews (Heb 6:5). It is also the subject of Paul's epistles "...the saints shall judge the world..." (1 Cor. 6:2). Peter also speaks of the world to come (2Peter 3:13) "...we ... look for a new heavens and a new earth wherein dwelleth righteousness." Paul refers to the world of angels when he speaks of the world to come (1Cor. 6:1-8). However, the Hebrew epistles (Hebrews through Revelation) refer to the world to come on this earth, as the seventh angel of Revelation 11:15 says; "...the kingdoms of this world are become the kingdoms of our Lord, and of his Christ, and he shall reign for ever and ever."

The book of Hebrews also makes the important point that the world to come will not be put into the hands of angels whereby angels would be the custodians of that world. Rather we learn from this passage that God's purpose in creating man in the beginning (Genesis 1) was to have the world of men and the world of angels to ultimately be in the hands of man as the eternal custodians of both. Revelation 5:11 speaks of Israel being a nation of kings and priests who will "...reign on the earth..." Members of the Body of Christ who are willing to suffer with Christ (2Tim. 2:10-13) will also reign with Christ. However, because our eternal abode will be in the heavens (2Cor. 5:1), we will reign in the heavens. So we see then that God has two separate and distinct elect agencies: the nation of Israel (which will reign on the earth) and the Church which is Christ's Body (which will reign with Him in the heavens). Both elect agencies are redeemed by the shed blood of Christ (Eph. 1:7, Col. 1:14, Heb. 9:12). It is by the shed blood of Christ that God reconciles all things (in heaven and on earth) back to Himself (2Cor. 5:18, Col. 1:20).

Verse 6 speaks of "One in a certain place..." That certain place is Psalm 8:4-8. It is also found in similar expressions in the following passages:

Job 7:17-18 (KJV)
¹⁷ What *is* man, that thou shouldest magnify him? and that thou shouldest set thine heart upon him? ¹⁸ And *that* thou shouldest visit him every morning, *and* try him every moment?

Job 15:14-16 (KJV)
¹⁴ What *is* man, that he should be clean? and *he which is* born of a woman, that he should be righteous? ¹⁵ Behold, he putteth no trust in his saints [angels]; yea, the heavens are not clean in his sight. ¹⁶ How much more abominable and filthy *is* man, which drinketh iniquity like water?

Psalm 144:3 (KJV)

³ LORD, what *is* man, that thou takest knowledge of him! or the son of man, that thou makest account of him!

The words "...that thou visitest him?" in Verse 6 focuses on the human race as the offspring of Adam. Man has been visited by God in the person of Jesus Christ the Son. Joseph's dying words to Israel in Egypt speak of God one day visiting the nation.

Genesis 50:24-25 (KJV)

²⁴ And Joseph said unto his brethren, I die: and <u>God will surely visit you</u>, and bring you out of this land unto the land which he sware to Abraham, to Isaac, and to Jacob. ²⁵ And Joseph took an oath of the children of Israel, saying, God will surely visit you, and ye shall carry up my bones from hence.

Zacharias, the father of John the Baptist said:

Luke 1:68-78 (KJV)

⁶⁸ Blessed *be* the Lord God of Israel; for <u>he hath visited and redeemed</u> his people, ⁶⁹ And hath raised up an horn of salvation for us in the house of his servant David; ⁷⁰ As he spake by the mouth of his holy prophets, which have been since the world began: ⁷¹ That we should be saved from our enemies, and from the hand of all that hate us; ⁷² To perform the mercy *promised* to our fathers, and to remember his holy covenant; ⁷³ The oath which he sware to our father Abraham, ⁷⁴ That he would grant unto us, that we being delivered out of the hand of our enemies might serve him without fear, ⁷⁵ In holiness and righteousness before him, all the days of our life. ⁷⁶ And thou, child, shalt be called the prophet of the Highest: for thou shalt go before the face of the Lord to prepare his ways; ⁷⁷ To give knowledge of salvation unto his people by the remission of their sins, ⁷⁸ Through the tender mercy of our God; whereby the dayspring [a reference to Christ] from on high <u>hath visited us,</u>..."

Note in Acts 15:14 James points out that God is today visiting the Gentiles to call out a people from them. This however, is a temporary visit. His natural home is with His nation of Israel. When He is done visiting the Gentiles to call out a people for the heavens, He will return to His nation again.

In Verse 7 we read "Thou madest him a little lower than the angels..." Here the focus is still on angels but now man comes in the picture as being made lower than the angels. In Verse 9, we see that Jesus was made lower than the angels. However, in Verse 9 we also see what that means. He was made lower that the angels "...for the suffering of death..." Men are lower than the angels in many ways but the primary focus here is on the fact that men can die (physically) while angels can't. Christ was made lower than the angels for the suffering of death. He had to be made lower than the angels when He entered humanity so that He could die as a man to pay man's sin debt.

Verse 8a reads "Thou hast put all things in subjection under his feet..." This is a reference to Adam and the entire human race through Adam. God created man as a free moral agent and commissioned him to have dominion over His creation (Gen. 1:28). However, man failed (in Adam) and lost the dominion over the works of God's hands. Therefore, God had to enter into the human race to do for man what man could not do for himself. It is now only through the redeeming work of Christ that the dominion of man over the earth will again be restored.

Daniel 7:13-14 (KJV) ¹³ I saw in the night visions, and, behold, *one* like the Son of man [Jesus] came with the clouds of heaven [angels], and came to the Ancient of days [the Father], and they brought him [Jesus] near before him. [14] And there was given him dominion, and glory, and a kingdom, that all people, nations, and languages, should serve him: his dominion *is* an everlasting dominion, which shall not pass away, and his kingdom *that* which shall not be destroyed.

Verse 8b goes on to say "...He left nothing that is not put under him..." In Genesis 1:28, the dominion that man was to have was a dominion that extended only to the earth (as far as what was revealed in Scripture at that time). However, when we come to the writings of Paul the apostle of the Gentiles, we find that God had a secret purpose in the creation of man that He never revealed until He saved Saul of Tarsus and commissioned him as "the apostle of the Gentiles" and revealed the mystery through him. The Mystery was simply that God would call out a body of believers called the church which is Christ's Body as the elect agency through whom He would extend man's dominion over "...all things whether they be things in earth, or things in heaven" (Col. 1:20). However, the only members of the human race who will have such dominion are those who have been reconciled to God by the shed blood of Christ (Col. 1:21-22).

Verse 8c brings it back to where we are at today -- "But now we see not yet all things put under him." We understand that Adam (and the son of Adam – the human race) was to reign (Gen. 1:28) but to this day man, in spite of all of his scientific accomplishments, still does not reign over creation as God originally intended. Rather, creation reigns over him (Gen 3:17-19). The creation over which man was to reign now reclaims man's body at death. All of creation waits for the day that man will be redeemed from the curse that was put on all of creation (Rom. 8:18-25). One day both man and creation will be delivered from the bondage of corruption into the glorious liberty of the children of God. (Rom. 8:21).

> **Hebrews 2: 9-10** "But we see Jesus, who was made a little lower than the angels for the suffering of death, crowned with glory and honour; that he by the grace of God should taste death for every man. [10] For it became him, for whom *are* all things, and by whom *are* all things, in bringing many sons unto glory, to make the captain of their salvation perfect through sufferings."

Today we do not see man being what he was created to be – the eternal custodians of God's creation. However, we do see (i.e. we see in the Word of God and in our spiritual experience of regeneration) Jesus crowned with glory and honor. There is one member of our human race who is what God intended man to be in the beginning. This takes us to the resurrection of the Lord Jesus Christ (1 Cor. 15:12-23). He did not have to be first made lower than the angels in order to be crowned with glory and honor because He had that from eternity past (John 17:5, Phil. 2:6-9). Here we see why and how Christ was made lower than the angels (that being for the suffering of death). Man can die. Angels (from what we see in scripture) do not die. Jesus is the promised Seed of the woman that would crush the serpent's head (Gen. 3:15) and thus undo the curse of death (both spiritually and physically – Gen. 2:17). Christ had to not only become a man but had to become a curse for us and die under the curse of sin in order to deliver us from that curse (Rom. 8:3, Gal. 3:13, 4:4-5; Isa. 53:2-11).

"...Crowned with glory and honor..." Jesus Christ is today exalted by the right hand of God (Acts 2:33) and will one day come back being "...crowned with many crowns..." (Rev. 19:12).

Verse 9 says "...That he by the grace of God should taste death for every man." We ask: "Why was it that Jesus was made lower than the angels?" The answer is: "That he by the grace of God should taste death for every man." In Isaiah 53:8 it was said that "...for the transgression of my [Isaiah's] people [Israel] was he [Christ] stricken." In Matthew 20:28 we see the Lord giving His life *a ransom for many*. In 1 Timothy 2:6 we find Christ "...gave himself *a ransom for all*, to be testified in due time." Until Paul comes on the scene as "the apostle of the Gentiles," Christ is seen only as the redeemer of Israel (Luke 1:68, 24:21; 2Sam. 7:23, Neh. 1:10, Isa. 52:9, 62:12). Today in the Dispensation of Grace we learn that "the righteousness of God" that everyone needs in order to enter into eternal life but which no one has in his own right, is available to everyone without distinction (Rom. 3:21-25, 2Cor. 5:21). Here in Hebrews, the writer again is presenting a salvation that is available for every man. However, the salvation to all in Hebrews through Revelation is a salvation that is available to all men through redeemed Israel. Israel is God's "chosen generation, a royal priesthood, a holy nation, a peculiar people." (1 Peter 2:9). The Circumcision epistles (Hebrews through Revelation) go back to the circumcised Abraham and the promise to him that "in thy seed shall all the nations of the earth be blessed..." (Gen. 22:18 cf. James 2:22). The apostle Paul goes back to the uncircumcised Abram of Genesis 17 (Rom. 4:9-14) and even back further than that to Adam (Rom. 5:17-21) when he speaks of redemption. In Galatians 3:26 we find that believers of the Dispensation of Grace are baptized into Jesus Christ and thereby they become Abraham's seed in Christ (which is Abraham's seed).

"It became him..." is used in Verse 10. The term "...it became him..." is used in the sense of a thing that is well-suited to His character. It was becoming of the creator to suffer in order to bring many sons to glory. In Genesis 18:25 when Abraham was pleading with the Lord to spare Lot he said, "that be far from thee... to slay the righteous with the wicked, and that the righteous should be as the wicked, that be far from thee: shall not the judge of all the earth do right?" Yet on Calvary, God allowed His righteous Son to die in the place of the wicked. There on Calvary, God was setting "...forth His Son to be a propitiation through faith in his blood, to declare his righteousness for the remission of sins that are past through the forbearance of God; to declare I say, at this time his righteousness: that he might be just and the justifier of him which believeth in Jesus" (Rom. 3:22-25). Note in this passage that the "faith" in Verse 23 is the Father's faith in the coming shed blood of His only begotten Son that allowed Him to remit the sins of the Old Testament saints. .

"For whom *are* all things, and by whom *are* all things..." in verse 10 speaks of Christ. The Apostle Paul says of Him: [16] For by him were all things created, that are in heaven, and that are in earth, visible and invisible, whether *they be* thrones, or dominions, or principalities, or powers: all things were created by him, and for him: [17] And he is before all things, and by him all things consist (Col. 1:16-17). The 24 elders of Revelation 24:11 say of Him: "[11] Thou art worthy, O Lord, to receive glory and honour and power: for thou hast created all things, and for thy pleasure they are and were created." (Rev. 4:11). Speaking of Israel, God says of them: "[21] This people have I formed for myself; they shall shew forth my praise. **(**Isaiah 43:21). Paul speaks of Christ in Romans 11:36: "For of him, and through him, and to him, *are* all things: to whom *be* glory for ever. Amen." He writes again in 1Corinthians 8:6: "But to us *there is but* one God, the Father, of whom *are* all things, and we in him; and one Lord Jesus Christ, by whom *are* all things, and we by him." He writes in 2 Corinthians 5:17-18 "[17] Therefore if any man *be* in Christ, *he is* a new creature: old things are passed away; behold, all things are become new. [18] And all things *are* of God, who hath reconciled us to himself by Jesus Christ, and hath given to us the ministry of reconciliation..."

"...In bringing many sons unto glory..." in Verse 10 There is much to be said and much to be wondered at in this statement. God has but one "only begotten Son." However, it is His intention to have many sons through Him. "As many as are led by the Spirit of God they are the sons of God... the Spirit itself beareth witness with our spirit that we are the children of God" (Rom. 8:14-16). "For whom he did foreknow, he also did predestinate to be conformed to the image of his Son that He might be the firstborn of many brethren." (Rom. 8:29) In the Old Testament, God referred to Israel as "My son" (Ex. 4:22). In John 11:50-52 Caiaphas prophesies "that one man [Christ] should die for the people, and that the whole nation perish not... And not for that nation only, but that also he should gather together in one the children of God that were scattered abroad."

The passage in 1John 3:1-3 speaks of the wonder of being a son of God: "Behold what manner of love the Father hath bestowed upon us, that we should be called the sons of God...Behold, now we are the sons of God, and it doth not yet appear what we shall be: but we know that, when he shall appear, we shall be like him; for we shall see him as he is." That was in reference to Israel. But God is today, in the Dispensation of Grace calling out sons from among the Gentiles by faith in Christ (Gal. 3:26) -- "...Having predestinated us to the adoption of children by Jesus Christ to himself, according to the good pleasure of his will." (Eph. 1:5). Today, God has expanded His family beyond Israel to include the Gentile believers of the dispensation of grace (2Cor. 6:18). The wonder of it all is not just that we can be sons of God in Christ, but that we can partake with Christ in the glory: "He is bringing many sons to glory." Peter says, "The elders which are among you I exhort, who am also an elder, and a witness of the sufferings of Christ, and also a partaker of the glory that shall be revealed." (1Peter 5:1) "But the God of all grace, who hath called us unto his eternal glory by Christ Jesus..." (1Peter 5:10) This glory that originally pertained only to Israel (Rom. 9:4) now extends to the Gentiles (Rom. 9:22-24) who are now members of the Body of Christ. It is the Mystery program that brings this glory to the Gentiles (1Cor. 2:7). Our light affliction (2Cor. 4:17) and the sufferings of today are not worthy to be compared with that glory (Rom. 8:18). It is only when Christ appears that we will see that glory (Col. 3:4).

"...To make the captain of their salvation perfect through sufferings..." in Verse 10 Jesus Christ is the captain of Israel's salvation in that He is the forerunner (Heb. 6:2) who as "...the High Priest after the order of Melchizedec..." will lead the nation as a kingdom of priests and a holy nation into the Kingdom of Heaven. Jesus is "... the author and finisher of *our* faith; who for the joy that was set before him endured the cross, despising the shame, and is set down at the right hand of the throne of God." (Heb. 12:2) Christ is the captain in the sense that He is Israel's leader who will lead the nation into the kingdom. Isaiah sees Him as Israel's commander: "...I have given him *for* a witness to the people, a leader and commander to the people. ⁵ Behold, thou shalt call a nation *that* thou knowest not, and nations *that* knew not thee shall run unto thee because of the LORD thy God, and for the Holy One of Israel; for he hath glorified thee." (Isa. 55:3-5)

Israel could have no part in the suffering for the atonement. However, Christ was made perfect (complete) as Israel's leader (Captain) by suffering to make atonement for the nation. It is after the suffering for atonement that God says of Christ "Him hath God exalted with his right hand *to be* a Prince and a Savior, for to give repentance to Israel, and forgiveness of sins." (Act 5:31)

> **Hebrews 2: 11-15** "For both he that sanctifieth and they who are sanctified *are* all of one: for which cause he is not ashamed to call them brethren, ¹²Saying, I will declare thy name unto my brethren, in the midst of the church will I sing praise unto thee. ¹³And again, I will put my trust in him. And again, Behold I and the children which God hath given me. ¹⁴Forasmuch then as the children are partakers of flesh and blood, he also himself likewise took part of the same; that through death he might destroy him that had the power of death, that is, the devil; ¹⁵ And deliver them who through fear of death were all their lifetime subject to bondage."

" For both he that sanctifieth and they who are sanctified *are* all of one:..." in Verse 11 This takes us back to John 17:21 where we see the Lord praying to the Father "That they all may be one; as thou, Father, *art* in me, and I in thee, that they also may be one in us: that the world may believe that thou hast sent me." The Lord is speaking of Israel being one with the Father and the Son.

When Paul comes on the scene of Scripture, we find God expanding the concept of oneness as God reaches out to the Gentiles with the Dispensation of Grace. Paul tells people on Mars Hill,

> "²⁴ God that made the world and all things therein, seeing that he is Lord of heaven and earth, dwelleth not in temples made with hands; ²⁵ Neither is worshipped with men's hands, as though he needed any thing, seeing he giveth to all life, and breath, and all things; ²⁶ And hath made of one blood all nations of men for to dwell on all the face of the earth, and hath determined the times before appointed, and the bounds of their habitation; ²⁷ That they should seek the Lord, if haply they might feel after him, and find him, though he be not far from every one of us: ²⁸ For in him we live, and move, and have our being; as certain also of your own poets have said, For we are also his offspring." Acts 17:24-28

"...For which cause he is not ashamed to call them brethren," The Lord entered humanity to be the captain of the salvation of man. Therefore, He is not ashamed that, though He is God, to nonetheless call men His brethren. Interestingly, though He is not ashamed to take on humanity, some of humanity is ashamed to associate with Him (Luke 9:26, Mark 8:38). The Lord sees His brethren being those members of our race who resolve to do the will of His Father (Matt. 12:48-50) and who indeed do it. We see in passages such as Matthew 25:40 how much He values His brethren. He freely referred to His disciples as brethren (Matt. 28:10, John 20:17). Today in the Dispensation of Grace, God is in the business of conforming us to the image of His Son that His Son might be the firstborn of many brethren (Rom. 8:29).

"Saying..." Verse 12 is a quote from Psalm 22:22 "I will declare thy name unto my brethren: in the midst of the congregation will I praise thee." Verse 13a is an allusion to passages as 2 Samuel 22:3 and Psalm 16:1: "Preserve me, O God: for in thee do I put my trust." Verse 13b is a reference back to Isaiah 8:18 "Behold, I and the children whom the LORD hath given me *are* for signs and for wonders in Israel from the LORD of hosts, which dwelleth in mount Zion." These verses are referring to the Lord's disciples and the believing remnant of Israel as brethren of the Lord and children of God. With that in mind, consider Isaiah 53:10: "Yet it pleased the LORD to bruise him; he hath put *him* to grief: when thou shalt make his soul an offering for sin, he shall see *his* seed, he shall prolong *his* days, and the pleasure of the LORD shall prosper in his hand." But Isaiah 53:8 asks, "...Who shall declare his generation? For he was cut out of the land of the living..." We note that He died before He had physical offspring – yet He had children (Isa. 53:10). His children are spiritual children of God and brethren of Christ.

"I and the children which God hath given me..." (Verse 13) The Lord refers to His disciples in John 10:29 saying: "My Father which gave them me is greater than all; and no man is able to pluck them out of my Father's hand. I and my Father are one." In His prayer to the Father, he said "I have manifested thy name unto the men which thou gavest me out of the world: thine they were and thou gavest them me; and they have kept thy word... And all mine are thine and thine are mine, and I am glorified in them. ...While I was with them in the world. I kept them in thy name, and none is lost but the son of perdition..." (John 17:6-12).

"He also himself likewise took part of the same..." (Verse 14) In other words, He took on flesh and blood. This is probably the greatest enigma of the Bible: that the Creator entered His creation to take on the form of men so that He as man can pay sin's debt on behalf of man.

- "Who being in the form of God...made himself of no reputation, and took upon him the form of a servant, and was made in the likeness of men..." (Phil. 2:6-8)
- "...God [sent] His Son in the likeness of sinful flesh." (Note it is not "as sinful flesh" but rather "in the likeness of sinful flesh" -- Rom. 8:3)
- Isaiah 7:14 "Therefore the Lord himself shall give you a sign; Behold, a virgin shall conceive, and bear a son,

and shall call his name Immanuel [God with us]."

"...that through death he might destroy him that had the power of death..." (Verse 14) It is not "the power over death" but the power of death. The Lord Jesus Christ has the power over death because He defeated death (1Cor. 15:26). Satan has the power of death in that he can control people by death (Rev. 2:10). Satan was a murderer (literally "man slayer") from the beginning (from the beginning of man – John 8:44). One day Christ will destroy death as Paul says: "...the last enemy that will be destroyed is death" (1Cor. 15:26). Isaiah 25:6-8 prophesies of a time when death will be swallowed up in victory in Israel's coming Messiah. However, Satan is the one who uses the fear of death (Heb. 2:15) to hold people in bondage. The fear of death is the fear of dying unprepared. This is the case of the man under law (Ezek. 18:24-26).

"Who through fear of death were all their lifetime subject to bondage..." (Verse 15) What bondage is this talking about? It is the bondage to the Law. We today are delivered from the bondage of the Law. Israel under their New Covenant will also be delivered from that bondage. One who knows that eternal life is a gift to be received by faith is set free to live the life of Christ. Such a one is not in bondage to make his or her flesh perform up to the standard of the Law (Gal. 4:3-10, 5:1-4). Rather than having the spirit of the fear of death working in us, we have "...the spirit of power and of love and of a sound mind." (2Tim. 1:7). The opposite of the spirit of fear is the spirit of adoption whereby we know that we are the children of God (Rom. 8:15, 21).

> **Hebrews 2:16-18** "For verily he took not on *him the nature of* angels; but he took on *him* the seed of Abraham. [17] Wherefore in all things it behoved him to be made like unto *his* brethren, that he might be a merciful and faithful high priest in things *pertaining* to God, to make reconciliation for the sins of the people. [18] For in that he himself hath suffered being tempted, he is able to succour them that are tempted."

Christ did not enter into the race of angels. Therefore, redemption is not offered to angels. God had a plan for the redemption of man before He created man (1Peter 1:20).

Christ took on him the seed of Abraham (Verse 16). Here in Hebrews the focus is not on the human race in Adam but on the seed of the circumcised Abraham (Gen. 22:18ff). This is the same focus that the four Gospel records have (Matt. 1:1). The Apostle Paul however focuses on the uncircumcised Abram (Rom. 4:16, Gal. 3:16, 24).

"In all things it behoved him to be made like unto *his* brethren..." (Verse 17) In verse 12 we saw that the brethren were the members of the congregation of which Psalm 22:22-25 speaks. Those brethren are the faithful members of the nation of Israel. The children are God's children. Therefore, being the only begotten Son, Christ could call the believing Israelites His brethren. Therefore, He is not ashamed to call them brethren because they are sanctified in Christ Himself (vs. 11).

"...That he might be a merciful and faithful high priest..." (Verse 17) Christ was made like His fellow men in order to be a faithful and merciful High Priest. Because He was tempted as we are, He is able to relate to us and can thus represent us before God. He was in all points tempted like we are yet without sin (Heb. 4:15). He is Israel's High Priest. A priest represents a third party before God. Christ was born as a seed of Abraham so as to represent the seed of Abraham (His brethren) before God. He could, as a high priest, be merciful in the sense that He knew what it was like to be tempted as His brethren were. He could also be faithful as a high priest in that, though tempted, He did not sin.

"…To make reconciliation for the sins of the people…" (Verse 17) His work as a high priest was to make reconciliation for the sins of the people. The phrase "to make reconciliation" literally means to make propitiation – a fully satisfying payment. Related Old Testament passages include: Leviticus 6:30; 8:15; 2Chronicales 29:24; Ezekiel 45:15,17, 20; and Daniel 9:24. These all pertain to Israel. We today have a reconciliation also: Romans 5:10; 2Corinthians 5:18-21; Ephesians 2:6; and Colossians 1:21 are passages that speak of ours. .

"…That he himself hath suffered being tempted, he is able to succour them that are tempted." (Verse 18) This temptation was not a temptation to do any evil work. James 1:13&14 says "Let no man say when he is tempted, I am tempted of God: for God cannot be tempted with evil, neither tempteth he any man: But every man is tempted when he is drawn away of his own lust, and enticed." This temptation of Christ is in the sense of trying Him to prove Him. Comparing Genesis 22:1 with Hebrews 11:17 with regard to Abraham being "tempted" and "tried" made this clear. God knew what was in Abraham's heart and did not have to "try" him. However, to give Israel an example of the kind of faith that they will need (one day) to get through the Tribulation Period, God "tempts" / "tries" Abraham. James cites Abraham's faith that was demonstrated by his work of offering his promised son as the example of how an Israelite is justified by works and not by faith only (James 2:24). Israel will be God's house "if we [they] hold fast the confidence and the rejoicing of the hope firm unto the end." (Heb. 3:6).

Table 2 The Threefold Temptation
Considering how He was tempted, we consider and compare three passages:

1John 2:16	Lust of the Flesh	Lust of the eyes	Pride of Life
Genesis 3:6	Good for food	Pleasant to the eyes	A tree to be desired to make one wise
Luke 1:1-13 Matt. 4:1-11	Command these stones to be made bread	Showed him all the kingdoms of the world	If thou be the Son of God cast thyself from hence: for it is written he shall give his angels charge over thee.

The Kinsman Redeemer

Hebrews Chapter 2 is to Israel what Romans Chapter 3 is to us in the Dispensation of Grace. Hebrews 2 presents Christ as Israel's Kinsman Redeemer. We find the concept presented in Leviticus 25:24-26, and 48-52. If an Israelite is sold into slavery, someone who is a close kin can redeem him to set him free. But there were qualifications to be a redeemer:

The kinsman redeemer:

1. Had to be close kin.
2. Had to be able to do it.
3. Had to be willing to do it.

Israel was enslaved to sin. Christ, to redeem Israel had to be an Israelite. He had to be free from sin Himself to be able to redeem Israel. He was willing to redeem Israel. Because He was an Israelite and because He cleared their sin's account, "He is not only their brother, but He is also not ashamed to call them brethren. Not only is He their Kinsman Redeemer, He is also the Captain of their salvation to take Israel into her inheritance as He did when He led Joshua into Israel's inheritance (Heb. 2:11-13 cf Josh. 5:14). As the Captain of their salvation, He had to be made perfect (or complete) by suffering and "taste death for every man" (Heb. 2:9). Christ was perfect as God and He lived a perfect life as a man but He still had to be made complete as the Kinsman Redeemer by dying for the sins of the people. Israel is the treasure hid in a field in Matthew 13:44. Christ redeems the field (i.e. the world) so that he can have the treasure –- the Kingdom. Therefore, He had to die to be complete as the Savior.

Study Guides Questions on Chapter 2

1. What is the first of a number of warnings in the Book of Hebrews?
2. To what does the term "spoken by angels" in Verse 2 refer?
3. When will Israel nationally receive the atonement?
4. What is the great salvation of which Verse 3 speaks?
5. Is there a difference between "the salvation which began to be spoken by the Lord" and the salvation that we have today?
6. Israel was delivered by blood in Egypt and by power in the crossing of the Red Sea. How are the books of Hebrews and the Revelation antitypes of these?
7. Verse 4 talks about signs, wonders, miracles, and gifts of the Spirit. Should we be looking for these witnesses too?
8. What, according to Verse 7, is God's purpose for creating man?
9. We don't see man today being what God created him to be. But what according to Verse 9 do we see?
10. In Verse 10 we see Jesus as creator and possessor of all things but He is also what?
11. How was Jesus perfected according to Verses 9 and 10?
12. How is Chapter 2 to the Hebrew people like Romans Chapter 3 to us?

CHAPTER 3
JESUS THE APOSTLE AND HIGH PRIEST

Hebrews 3:1-2 "Wherefore, holy brethren, partakers of the heavenly calling, consider the Apostle and High Priest of our profession, Christ Jesus; ² Who was faithful to him that appointed him, as also Moses *was faithful* in all his house."

The words "Wherefore, holy brethren..." in Verse one means that the writer identifies himself with "the children..." who "...are partakers of flesh and blood..." (Heb. 2:14) He also identifies with the members of the human race that God entered into in the person of Christ (Heb. 2:17). The writer also associates himself with the Savior (Heb. 2:14), with the seed of Abraham (Heb. 2:16), and even with all men (Heb. 2:6). They are "holy" brethren in that they have been set apart as God's unique possession. This takes us to 1Peter 2:9 where Peter writes to the dispersion (1Peter 1:1) saying "...ye are a chosen generation, a royal priesthood, an holy nation, a peculiar people; that ye should show forth the praise of him who hath called you out of darkness into his marvelous light."

He identifies the readers as "...partakers of the heavenly calling..." The heavenly calling here is what Peter calls "the glory that shall be revealed..." in 1Peter 5:1. This is a reference to the kingdom of heaven that will be set up on the earth. The establishment of that kingdom of heaven on the earth has been temporarily interrupted by the Dispensation of Grace. Peter learned of that interruption from Paul to whom the Lord revealed the information regarding the Dispensation of Grace and the entire program that God is administering throughout this present dispensation. We see when Peter gained this information by comparing his first epistle with his second. In 1Peter 4:7 Peter says, "...the end of all things is at hand..." envisioning that the Kingdom of Heaven is about to be established. However, in 2Peter 3:1-18 Peter (having received the information from Paul regarding the Dispensation of Grace temporarily interrupting the prophetic program) writes, "⁹ The Lord is not slack concerning his promise, as some men count slackness; but is longsuffering to us-ward, not willing that any should perish, but that all should come to repentance. ¹⁰ But the day of the Lord will come as a thief in the night; in the which the heavens shall pass away with a great noise, and the elements shall melt with fervent heat, the earth also and the works that are therein shall be burned up." (2Peter 3:9-10). Peter then directs his hearers to Paul's epistles to understand why the Kingdom of Heaven has not yet been established on earth (2Peter 3:15). What intervened between First Peter and Second Peter was the Jerusalem conference of Acts 15. When we go to Paul's epistles, we see that the prophetic program with Israel has been temporarily interrupted with the Dispensation of Grace. "²⁵ For I would not, brethren, that ye should be ignorant of this mystery, lest ye should be wise in your own conceits; that blindness in part is happened to Israel, until the fulness of the Gentiles be come in. ²⁶ And so all Israel shall be saved: as it is written, There shall come out of Sion the Deliverer, and shall turn away ungodliness from Jacob: ²⁷ For this *is* my covenant unto them, when I shall take away their sins. ²⁸ As concerning the gospel, *they are* enemies for your sakes: but as touching the election, *they are* beloved for the fathers' sakes. ²⁹ For the gifts and calling of God *are* without repentance." (Rom. 11:25-29)

God is "the God of heaven..." today (Dan. 2:44). But He will one day set up a Kingdom upon the earth in which His will shall be done on the earth as it is in heaven (Matt. 6:9). Today though, the Kingdom rests with the King, who is in exile in heaven. The parables of Matthew 25:14 and Luke 19:22 refer to the Lord returning back to heaven, then one day returning again to the earth to set up the promised Kingdom.

The inheritance for the kingdom saints is there in heaven where it is vested in the King (1Peter 1:3-4). The reward for faithfulness on the part of kingdom saints is reserved in Heaven with the King (Matt. 5:12, Luke 6:23, 10:20, 12:3,

Rev. 22:12). The believing remnant of Israel (those believing Israelites in Acts Chapters 1 thru 7) experienced "the heavenly gift..." as a foretaste of the Kingdom (Heb. 6:4). The Old Covenant was a shadow of the heavenly things of the New Covenant yet to come (Heb. 8:5). Christ, after shedding His blood, entered the heavenly holy place (Heb. 9:22ff) as Israel's High Priest. The city that Abraham looked for is in the heavens today (Heb. 11:10). Though the city is in heaven today, it will come down from heaven to the earth (Rev. 3:12 and 21:2) or at least in the vicinity of the earth, one day (Rev. 7:16). The heavenly country that they looked for will be established on earth (Heb. 11:16).

Paul refers to "a heavenly kingdom" in 2 Timothy 4:8. This is in contrast to the term "the kingdom of heaven" which refers to a kingdom set up upon the earth. This heavenly kingdom that Paul refers to in his epistles is a kingdom in heaven where our resurrection bodies (for members of the body of Christ – the church of the Dispensation of Grace) will be (2Cor. 5:1).

Verse 1 refers to the "Apostle and High Priest of our profession..." An apostle is one sent. Christ was sent by the Father to Israel to be Israel's High Priest. This statement introduces the high priestly work of Israel's Messiah as prophesied in the Old Testament (Psalm 110:1-4). This is the theme of the book of Hebrews as evidenced by the many passages on the subject in the book (Heb. 2:17, 4:14-15, 5:1-10, 6:20, 7:26, 8:1-3, 9:11, 10:21).

Note the flow of thought in the book so far. Each chapter has a different presentation of the ministry of Christ:

- Chapter 1 – the Son of God
- Chapter 2 – the Son of Man
- Chapter 3 – The Apostle and High Priest of our Profession
- Chapter 4 – the Antitype of Joshua who leads Israel into rest

A note on the dispensational changes taking place here is in order. Paul, through whom the Lord Jesus Christ reveals the Mystery, tells us that the things of the Old Testament are a shadow of things to come. This speaks of things that are future from where we are at today (Col 2:16-17). The Law will be fulfilled at a time after the Dispensation of Grace closes when the Kingdom is set up. Hebrews talks about that fulfillment.

> **Hebrews 3:3-6** "For this *man* was counted worthy of more glory than Moses, inasmuch as he who hath builded the house hath more honour than the house. [4] For every house is builded by some *man*; but he that built all things *is* God. [5] And Moses verily *was* faithful in all his house, as a servant, for a testimony of those things which were to be spoken after; [6] But Christ as a son over his own house; whose house are we, if we hold fast the confidence and the rejoicing of the hope firm unto the end.

These verses (3 thru 6) are not easy reading. The writer is contrasting that which Moses was head over with what Jesus Christ is head over. Verse 2 talks about a house over which Moses was appointed as a servant. Verse 3 says that God built the house over which Moses was appointed. The house is Israel. Christ is appointed as the High Priest over the house of Israel but not over the house of Israel under the Old Covenant given through Moses. The reference to "house" is actually to the house-law. There was a house-law given through Moses. There is to be a new house-law for Israel in the Kingdom reign of Christ. That house-law will not be the Old Covenant given through Moses but the New Covenant through the blood of Christ. There are three houses (or house laws) that can be identified in Scripture. Each of those houses had a set of blue prints given to a man by God.

1. There was the house over which Moses was appointed. The blueprints given for that House of Israel is the Law of Moses.

2. Jesus Christ is the Apostle and High Priest of the house of Israel under the New Covenant (Zech. 12:10-14, 1Peter 2:5-7). The Hebrews church epistles of Hebrews through Revelation present the blueprints for that house.

3. There is yet another house law in the Scripture – that being the Dispensation of the Grace of God that was given by Christ to and through Paul. The Pauline epistles comprise the blueprints for that house (1Cor. 3:10; Eph. 2:2; 3:1-5).

"Whose house are we, if…" Israel (the Hebrews) did not enjoy the absolute security as we do today in the Dispensation of Grace (Eph. 1:13). Israel is warned to hold fast their rejoicing of hope firm unto the end. Other similar verses include: 2Peter 1:10, Matthew 10:22, 24:13, Mark 13:13, Hebrews. 6:4, and 10:26ff. Israel's salvation will be different from ours. We have a complete spiritual salvation the moment we believe the gospel, with a physical salvation to follow when the rapture takes place. Israel, however, will have a physical salvation when the Lord returns to save them at the close of the Tribulation Period with a spiritual salvation to follow on Israel's real Day of Atonement when the New Covenant takes effect for the nation. Israel's deliverance from Egypt was a type of the deliverance that the nation will have in the Tribulation Period. Just as the nation that came out of Egypt was a mix of believers and unbelievers, so the nation in the Tribulation Period will again be such a mix. It was the same at Pentecost. The "end" that Verse 6 speaks of is the end of the Tribulation Period (and the end of the Gentile world dominion over the earth and the entrance into the Kingdom -- Matthew 24:3). Hebrews 6:11 is a reference to the same "end." The "end" will come when Israel will be able to say "The kingdoms of this world are become the kingdoms of our Lord and of His Christ." (Rev. 11:15). There are many passages in the Book of Daniel that look forward to this "end" (Dan. 7: 24ff, 8:17-19, 9:26ff, 11:35; and 12:4, 9, 13).

> **Hebrews 3:7-12** "[7]Wherefore (as the Holy Ghost saith, To day if ye will hear his voice, [8] Harden not your hearts, as in the provocation, in the day of temptation in the wilderness: [9] When your fathers tempted me, proved me, and saw my works forty years. [10] Wherefore I was grieved with that generation, and said, They do alway err in *their* heart; and they have not known my ways. [11] So I sware in my wrath, They shall not enter into my rest.) [12] Take heed, brethren, lest there be in any of you an evil heart of unbelief, in departing from the living God."

The "wherefore" of Verse 7 takes us back to the warning of Verse 6 and also ahead to the exhortation of Verse 12. The intervening parenthesis takes the reader back to the exodus from Egypt. The parenthesis is a quote from Psalm 95: 7-11. The Holy Ghost is applying this passage to Pentecost and the coming Tribulation Period (when Israel will again be at the same point of decision). Hosea 2:14-15 draws a parallel between Israel in the wilderness wanderings and the nation at Pentecost and the Tribulation. Note how the "today" of Verse 7 and Verse 13 draw the two events together. Just as the unbeliever was being purged from Israel in the wilderness, so the unbeliever will be purged from Israel in the Tribulation Period. So also, just as the generation that came out of Egypt did not go into the land, so too the generation to which the Holy Ghost witnessed at Pentecost did not go into the Kingdom. In both cases, the failure of that generation was "an evil heart of unbelief" and the "deceitfulness of sin." The Lord was grieved with that generation because "they have not known my ways." (vs. 10) Because they did "alway err in their heart…" God did "sware in my [His] wrath, they shall not enter into my rest." Entering into His rest is a reference to entering the kingdom. There are three significant rests that we find in scripture:

1. God rested on the seventh day of creation (Genesis 2:1).
2. There was the rest for Israel in the land of Canaan (Exodus).
3. There is the Kingdom rest for Israel (Hebrews).

Note in Verse 12 that "an evil heart of unbelief..." is equated with "departing from God..." They once were with God but they departed.

> **Hebrews 3:13-16** " But exhort one another daily, while it is called Today; lest any of you be hardened through the deceitfulness of sin. [14] For we are made partakers of Christ, if we hold the beginning of our confidence stedfast unto the end; [15] While it is said, To day if ye will hear his voice, harden not your hearts, as in the provocation. [16] For some, when they had heard, did provoke: howbeit not all that came out of Egypt by Moses.

In Verse 14 we see that there is a condition on being a partaker of Christ -- "If we hold the beginning of our confidence stedfast unto the end;... Here we again have that warning – the second warning that we find in Hebrews.

> **Hebrews 3:17-19** "But with whom was he grieved forty years? *was it* not with them that had sinned, whose carcases fell in the wilderness? [18] And to whom sware he that they should not enter into his rest, but to them that believed not? [19]

The Second Warning (Hebrews 3:17 – 4:13) -- Don't have an evil heart of unbelief as did Israel in the wilderness

So we see that they could not enter in because of unbelief. Israel as a nation faced the same consequences to their unbelief at Pentecost as the nation faced at Kadesh (Num. 13:26)

Study Guides Questions on Chapter3

1. What is the heavenly calling of which verse 1 speaks? Is this the same as the heavenly kingdom of 2Timothy 4:8?
2. Christ is head over His house in what capacity?
3. What is the condition that verse 6 places on Israel in order to be Christ's house?
4. The "today" of verses 7 and 13 draw two events together. What are they?
5. What is the rest that verse 7 talks about?
6. What condition does verse 14 place on Israel being partakers of Christ?

CHAPTER 4
A BETTER REST FOR THE PEOPOLE OF GOD

There ia a Better Rest for the Believer

Hebrews 4 1-5 "Let us therefore fear, lest, a promise being left *us* of entering into his rest, any of you should seem to come short of it. [2] For unto us was the gospel preached, as well as unto them: but the word preached did not profit them, not being mixed with faith in them that heard *it*. [3] For we which have believed do enter into rest, as he said, As I have sworn in my wrath, if they shall enter into my rest: although the works were finished from the foundation of the world. [4] For he spake in a certain place of the seventh *day* on this wise, And God did rest the seventh day from all his works. [5] And in this *place* again, If they shall enter into my rest."

The "therefore" takes us back to 3:17-19 where the writer talks about those that died in the wilderness who did not enter into Canaan rest because of unbelief. The "fear" of verse 1 is the fear of God that compels one to recognize God's power and authority. God said what He meant and meant what He said. We all must come to God on His terms. He administers His Salvation His way. The cause for fear is that though a promise is left to the Hebrews to enter into rest, some should seem to come short. The promise (and the rest) is the New Covenant and the Kingdom. The promise is the covenant (the New Covenant) and the rest is the kingdom.

"[40] And I will make an everlasting covenant with them, that I will not turn away from them, to do them good; but I will put my fear in their hearts, that they shall not depart from me." Jeremiah 32:40 (KJV)

In Verse 2 the writer is drawing a comparison of the Hebrews in his audience and the Hebrews that came out of Egypt. Both had gospel preached to them. In both cases some believed and others did not. In the earlier case (those coming out of Egypt), the believers entered into Canaan rest while the unbelievers endured the wrath of God. The good news preached to the Hebrews that came out of Egypt was that God was going to bring them into the Promised Land. The good news preached to the Hebrews here in the book of Hebrews is that God was going to bring them into the Kingdom but they first had to go on to perfection (Heb. 6:1) and not draw back unto perdition (Heb. 10:38-39, John 17:12, 2Thess. 2:3). The gospel of the Promised Land was preached to a generation of Hebrews in the Exodus but it did not profit most of them in that most of them did not believe it -- at least not enough to believe that they could defeat the giants in the land.

The Gospel of the Kingdom was preached to the Hebrews in Matthew, Mark, Luke, John and early Acts. However, we now know that they (for the most part) did not believe it. Paul says of them: "[3] For what if some did not believe? shall their unbelief make the faith of God without effect? [4] God forbid: yea, let God be true, but every man a liar; as it is written, That thou mightest be justified in thy sayings, and mightest overcome when thou art judged." Romans 3:3-4 (KJV)

"[3] **For we which have believed do enter into rest**..." God has rest for His people but it takes faith to enter into it. Some will enter by faith and others won't (Isaiah 65:11-16, Matt. 21:43-44, 22:10).

"[16] Thus saith the LORD, Stand ye in the ways, and see, and ask for the old paths, where *is* the good way, and walk therein, and ye shall find rest for your souls. But they said, We will not walk *therein*." Jeremiah 6:16 (KJV)

"²⁸ Come unto me, all *ye* that labour and are heavy laden, and I will give you rest. ²⁹ Take my yoke upon you, and learn of me; for I am meek and lowly in heart: and ye shall find rest unto your souls. ³⁰ For my yoke *is* easy, and my burden is light." (Matt. 11;28-30)

Verse 4 alludes to the seventh day of creation week (Gen. 1:31, 2:1-2) as a rest to make the point that rest comes when the work is done. There is a reference to work that leads to rest. One such work is the Lord's work of redemption that He accomplished on Calvary. The words in verse 5 "in this place again…" is a reference to Hebrews 3:11 and 4:9 that "there remaineth a rest for the people of God."

> **Hebrews 4:6-10** "Seeing therefore it remaineth that some must enter therein, and they to whom it was first preached entered not in because of unbelief: ⁷ Again, he limiteth a certain day, saying in David, To day, after so long a time; as it is said, To day if ye will hear his voice, harden not your hearts. ⁸ For if Jesus had given them rest, then would he not afterward have spoken of another day. ⁹ There remaineth therefore a rest to the people of God. ¹⁰ For he that is entered into his rest, he also hath ceased from his own works, as God *did* from his."

Verse 6 makes it clear that there is still a rest for the people of God in the future from the time of the writing of the Book of Hebrews.

Verse 7 is a reference to David in Psalm 95:7-11. The term "Today after so long a time…" is conveying the idea that the nation has in the past and will again in the future face the same situation of tempting the Lord but only some of the nation will pass the test and not harden their hearts. These (the believers) will go into the rest of the kingdom.

Verse 8 is a reference to Joshua taking Israel into the Promised Land (Josh 1:15, 22:4, Deut. 12:9, 25:19) "For if Jesus [Joshua] had given them rest, then would he not afterward have spoken of another day.". The writer is pointing out that there is still another rest ahead for them beyond that rest of Canaan. **Verse 9** speaks of the future rest for those who enter the kingdom.

> **Hebrews 4:11-13** "¹¹Let us labour therefore to enter into that rest, lest any man fall after the same example of unbelief. ¹² For the word of God *is* quick, and powerful, and sharper than any twoedged sword, piercing even to the dividing asunder of soul and spirit, and of the joints and marrow, and *is* a discerner of the thoughts and intents of the heart. ¹³ Neither is there any creature that is not manifest in his sight: but all things *are* naked and opened unto the eyes of him with whom we have to do."

One has to labor to enter into this rest. God rested from His work in creation (Gen. 1:31). He also rested from His work of redemption (John 19:30) when He said, "It is finished." So too, the tribulation saints will have to labor to enter the kingdom rest (see 1Peter 4:1-2). Peter speaks of this labor in 2Peter 1:10-11 "¹⁰ Wherefore the rather, brethren, give diligence to make your calling and election sure: for if ye do these things, ye shall never fall: ¹¹ For so an entrance shall be ministered unto you abundantly into the everlasting kingdom of our Lord and Saviour Jesus Christ." However, for us living in the Dispensation of Grace the situation is reversed. We are given eternal life as a gift (Rom. 6:23, Eph. 2:8-9) but then we labor because we are justified by grace, (Eph. 2:10, Phil. 2:12). We today labor after having received the gift by faith as an act of appreciation (2Cor. 5:14) for the gift of eternal life.

Verse 11 "...Lest any man fall after the same example of unbelief." The example of unbelief in view here is the unbelief of Israel at Kadesh-barnea. From Roman 11:12 and Romans 11:28-30 we know that many in Israel had fallen after the same example and we Gentiles today have the blessings of the Dispensation of Grace as a result.

Verse 12 "For the word of God *is* quick, and powerful..." The Word of God is quick (alive) because the Holy Ghost who gave it (2Peter 1:21) is ever present to minister it to believing hearts (Rom. 1:16, 1Thess. 2:13). The Word of God is powerful for the same reason -- it is the Sword of the Spirit (Eph. 6:17). It is the only real offensive weapon that we have in our arsenal for the spiritual conflict in which we find ourselves today (2Cor. 10:4-5). God's Word will not return to Him void (Isa. 55:11) – it will accomplish what God determined it to do. God tells Jeremiah that His Word is like a fire that consumes the chaff and like a hammer that breaks the rock (Jer. 23:29). Here the Word is said to be sharper than any two edged sword in that it can differentiate between the soul and spirit (something that no man can do aside from the enlightening effect of the Word of God) and that it is the discerner of the thoughts and intents of the heart. This aspect of the Word of God is being made here because the Hebrew people have a promise of rest in the Word and are being asked to discern the thoughts and intents of their hearts in the matter of trusting Jesus Christ as Israel's High Priest. The Word is calling them to believe to the saving of their souls.

Note on Verse 12

The issue in Hebrews is belief (faith). It is the Word of God that provides faith. In 1Thessalonians 2:13 "the word effectually worketh..." (this is the same word as is translated "powerful" in Hebrews 4:12). The Word of God distinguishes between the soul and the spirit. In the Old Testament scriptures, the soul and the body are often viewed as one entity. Leviticus 5:1-2 and 22:6 are examples of this. In Genesis 35:18 we see that the soul leaves the body at physical death. In James 2:26 we see that the spirit also leaves the body at death. In the New Testament scriptures, the distinction between the two (soul and spirit) is more clearly drawn.

In John 3:5 "Except a man [soul] be born of water [physical] and the Spirit [a spiritual birth] he cannot enter the Kingdom of God." Compare that with John 3:3 which says "Except a man be born again he can not see the Kingdom of God." There is a difference between seeing the kingdom and entering it. To "see it" is to see with the mind's eye – to understand. It takes a regenerated spirit to "see" the kingdom of God. It takes both a physical birth (into the nation of Israel) and spiritual birth (belief in the person and work of Christ as Messiah) to enter the Kingdom. Peter refers to this when he says that "...According to his abundant mercy hath begotten us again unto a lively hope by the resurrection of Jesus Christ from the dead" (1 Pet 1:3).

Verse 13 "...Naked and opened unto the eyes of him with whom we have to do." In Verse 12 the subject is the Word of God. In Verse 13 the pronoun refers to God. Here as in many other places, God sets His Word equal to Himself (e.g. Gal. 3:8). Both God and His Word search the thoughts and the intents of the Heart (1Chr. 28:9). God looks at the heart (1Sam. 16:7) and searches the heart (1Chr. 28:9) and the Word does the same thing. It is futile to think that we an hide anything from God.

Believers Kept in Perfect Peace

> **Hebrews 4: 14-16** "Seeing then that we have a great high priest, that is passed into the heavens, Jesus the Son of God, let us hold fast *our* profession. [15] For we have not an high priest which cannot be touched with the feeling of our infirmities; but was in all points tempted like as *we are, yet* without sin. [16] Let us therefore come boldly unto the throne of grace, that we may obtain mercy, and find grace to help in time of need."

Verse 14 introduces the main focus of the book of Hebrews – Jesus Christ as the great High Priest to Israel. Because they have such a High Priest, they need to hold fast their profession of faith. Israel's High Priest can be touched by the feeling of their infirmities because He is both God and man. As a reminder of the structure of the book so far:

In Chapter 1 He is presented as God.

In Chapter 2 He is presented as man.

In Chapter 3 He is presented as the Captain of their salvation – as the real Joshua who led Israel through the wilderness.

In Chapter 4 and on He is the High Priest that will lead Israel into the Kingdom.

Compare this with the four Branch titles of Christ:

- The Servant -- Zechariah 3:8 "Behold ...my Servant the Branch" Mark presents Him as the servant of the Lord.
- The King -- Jeremiah 23:5 "...I will raise up unto David a righteous Branch, and a king shall reign and prosper ... (cf. 33:15) Isaiah 11:1 "The Branch out of ... of Jesse" Matthew presents Him as the rightful king.
- The Man -- Zechariah 6:12 "Behold the man whose name is the Branch." Luke presents Him as the perfect man.
- God -- Isaiah 4:2 "The Branch of the Lord" John presents Him as God in human flesh.

Today Israel's High Priest is behind the veil in the sanctuary in heaven. One day He will come out from behind the veil to bring Israel her real Day of Atonement. Every time the Day of Atonement was celebrated by Israel in the Old Testament, they were acting out their prophetic future of this real Day of Atonement when Christ returns to deliver Israel. Peter looks forward to that day when "...your sins may be blotted out, when the times of refreshing shall come from the presence of the Lord...whom the heaven must receive until the times of restitution of all things, which God hath spoken by the mouth of all his prophets since the world began." (Acts 3:19-21). Jesus Christ is behind the veil today as the Head of the Church the Body of Christ but He is also there as the guarantor of Israel's future hope. Israel will have her future glory when Christ returns to bring it to them.

"[16] Let us therefore come boldly unto the throne of grace, that we may obtain mercy..." Israel's throne of grace is the heavenly mercy seat where the Lord Jesus Christ took His own blood. The mercy seat on earth is described in Exodus Chapter 25. It is there at the mercy seat where God met with men in Israel's Old Testament temple (Psalm 80:1, 99:1). It was there that the blood was applied on the Day of Atonement and it was there that God met with men. Both God and men are represented in the person of Jesus Christ who is the High Priest.

"...and find grace to help in time of need." Israel needed to find grace. They will find this grace in the Tribulation Period (James 4:6-8, 1Peter 1:3-6) in Christ as her High Priest. This book of Hebrews will be the basic instruction for them by which they will find this grace. Note the contrast of Israel's access to God through her high priest and ours in Christ as the Head of the Body of Christ (Eph. 2:18). What Israel has in Christ as her High Priest, we as members of the Body of Christ have by virtue of being in Christ according to the revelation of the Mystery (Eph. 3:1-10, Rom. 16:25). Note that it is the work of the Holy Spirit in baptizing us today into the death, burial and resurrection of Christ (Romans 6:1-6) that does for us what the high priestly work of Christ will do for Israel.

Study Guides Questions on Chapter 4

1. Who are the two groups of people in view in verse 2 and 3?
2. What "Good News" (Gospel) was preached to each of these two groups?
3. What Gospel was preached to the Hebrews in Matthew, Mark, Luke and John?
4. What rest does verse 4 allude to? What point is being made?
5. Why the reference to King David's words in verse 7?
6. Verse 11 suggests that the Hebrews had to labor in order to enter into rest. Did you have to labor to enter into the rest of salvation of your soul?
7. What does Verse 7 say about the Word of God?
8. What, according to verse 14, is the main focus of the Book of Hebrews?
9. How does each of the first four chapters present Christ?
10. How does each relate to the four branch titles?
11. Where is Israel's High Priest today?
12. What are the two immutable things in verse 18?

CHAPTER 5
THE GREAT HIGH PRIEST

Hebrews 5: 1-3 "For every high priest taken from among men is ordained for men in things *pertaining* to God, that he may offer both gifts and sacrifices for sins: ² Who can have compassion on the ignorant, and on them that are out of the way; for that he himself also is compassed with infirmity. ³ And by reason thereof he ought, as for the people, so also for himself, to offer for sins."

"For every high priest taken from among men..." Every priest has some characteristics common with every other priest. They are:

1. They were taken from among men.
2. They represent men before God and offer sacrifices for sin.
3. They are selected by God (vs. 4)
   - God selected Aaron and his sons in the Aaronic order.
   - God selected Christ in the order of Melchisedec.
4. They all offer gifts and sacrifices for sins of men.
5. They can have compassion on the ignorant and on them that are out of the way... That is, they can relate to the infirmities of men being men themselves.

Hebrews 5:4-6 " And no man taketh this honour unto himself, but he that is called of God, as *was* Aaron. ⁵ So also Christ glorified not himself to be made an high priest; but he that said unto him, Thou art my Son, to day have I begotten thee. ⁶ As he saith also in another *place*, Thou *art* a priest for ever after the order of Melchisedec."

Christ did not take to Himself the title of High Priest but was called of God the Father to that office. He occupies three offices in Israel:

1. He is a Prophet (Deut. 18:15,18-19, 7:34, Acts 3:22)
2. He is their High Priest (Psalm 110:4)
3. He is their King (Jer. 23:5)

The begetting of verse 5 was done on the day of His resurrection. We see that by comparing Psalm 2:6-7 with Acts 13:3-4. In Acts 13 we see Paul's address to the Jews at a Synagogue in Pisidian, Antioch. He tells them, "³³ God hath fulfilled the same unto us their children, in that he hath raised up Jesus again; as it is also written in the second psalm, Thou art my Son, this day have I begotten thee. ³⁴ And as concerning that he raised him up from the dead, *now* no more to return to corruption, he said on this wise, I will give you the sure mercies of David." (Acts 13:33-34, cf. Isa. 55:3) While He was on earth, He could not be a high priest because He was not of the tribe of Levi. Though during His earthly ministry He was the only begotten Son of God, He is not officially begotten as a Priest until His resurrection.

Hebrews 5:6 quotes Psalm 110:4. Psalm 110:1-10 speaks of the Messiah. "The LORD said unto my Lord, Sit thou at my right hand, until I make thine enemies thy footstool." This sets the time frame of the Psalm as being between His ascension to the Father's right hand and His return to earth to reign. It is during this time period that he is carrying out His High Priestly function to Israel. He was begotten to that function at His resurrection and He entered it at His ascension.

"Thou *art* a priest for ever..." He is a High Priest forever because the New Covenant will last forever. In Luke 18:30 we see that to enter into the Kingdom was to enter into "life everlasting." In Mark 10:17 the rich young ruler understood that to enter the Kingdom was to inherit "eternal Life." To be a priest forever is to be a priest who has eternal life. His eternal life is resurrection life.

"...after the order of Melchisedec..." This new priesthood has an Old Testament type in the man Melchisedec.

> **Hebrews 5: 7-10** "Who in the days of his flesh, when he had offered up prayers and supplications with strong crying and tears unto him that was able to save him from death, and was heard in that he feared; [8] Though he were a Son, yet learned he obedience by the things which he suffered; [9] And being made perfect, he became the author of eternal salvation unto all them that obey him; [10] Called of God an high priest after the order of Melchisedec."

"...He offered up prayers...unto him that was able to save him from death..." Note that He was not praying to be saved from dying. He was willing to die. What He had concern over was being saved from "death". The only salvation from death is resurrection. Peter says in Acts 2:24 that "It was not possible that death could hold Him." He was obedient unto death (Phil. 2:8). He was saved from death by rising from the dead. Christ willingly laid down His life (John 10:18, Matt. 26:53) in the confidence that His Father would do what He promised He would do – raise Him from the dead. Understanding this, we can better understand the travail of His soul in the Garden in Matthew 26:39.

Though he were a Son, yet..." This is interesting. He had to learn obedience to the Father. The obedience that He had to learn was obedience unto death (Phil. 2:8). He was officially begotten as a Son on the day of His resurrection (see note above). During His earthly ministry, He lived His life being totally dependent on the Father in heaven (John 5:30, cf. John 14:25 & 15:15). He then tells His disciples that they must in turn live their lives in total dependence on Him. He tells them that they can only bear fruit if they abide in Him (John 15:5). We today must learn the same truth if we are to bear fruit (Gal. 2:20, Phil. 3:9).

"...Being made perfect..." The word "perfect" has the thought of being made complete. He became complete as a Savior and High Priest by the things that He suffered. The things that He suffered were the shedding of His blood and dying as a sacrifice for sin. These are what made Him complete as a High Priest. Until He suffered these things He could not be made perfect as a High Priest. The basic function of a priest is to come to God with a sacrifice. The sacrifice that Christ offered was the surrender of His own perfect life. However, having made these sacrifices (the things that He suffered and the shedding of His own blood), He became the author of eternal salvation unto all them that obey Him. He was then called of God as a High Priest after the order of Melchisedec.

> **Hebrews 5:11-14** "Of whom we have many things to say, and hard to be uttered, seeing ye are dull of hearing. [12] For when for the time ye ought to be teachers, ye have need that one teach you again which *be* the first principles of the oracles of God; and are become such as have need of milk, and not of strong meat. [13] For every one that useth milk *is* unskillful in the word of righteousness: for he is a babe. [14] But strong meat belongeth to them that are of full age, *even* those who by reason of use have their senses exercised to discern both good and evil.

The Third Warning (3:17 – 4:13)

This is the third warning in the Book of Hebrews. The writer tells these Hebrews that they are dull of hearing. This takes us back to what the Lord told his disciples about the nation in Matthew 13:13 "Therefore speak I unto them in parables: because they seeing see not; and hearing hear not, neither do they understand." Here in the Book of Hebrews the time had come for them to understand but they are still dull of hearing. This has been a recurrent situation in Israel (Jer. 5:21, Ezek. 12:2, Matt. 13:15). The expression "He that hath an ear to hear let him hear…" is used eight times in the Book of the Revelation – once to each of the seven churches. The sum total of the information to the churches will give Israel the information on how to get through the Tribulation and into the Kingdom. The Israelite who does not have an ear to hear will be purged out of the nation and will therefore not get into the Kingdom. Several passages in John's gospel teach the importance of the hearing ear to Israel (John 8:30-40; 10:1-31).

John Chapter 10 presents the importance of hearing His voice. This passage in John warrants some careful attention.

- The sheepfold is a reference to the Little Flock in Israel
- The door into that sheepfold (Little Flock) is water baptism – typifying confession of sin and a need for cleansing.
- John the Baptizer is the porter that opens that door to the sheepfold.
- The shepherd Himself (Christ) comes through that same door (He was also baptized by John – Matt. 3:4) typifying His identification with the transgressors of Israel.
- The leaders of Israel who try to lead the sheep any other way than by water baptism are thieves and robbers (John 10:1 cf. Luke 7:29-30).
- The porter opens the door to the shepherd.
- The sheep hear the Shepherd's voice and they follow Him (John 10:3).
- The Lord refers to other sheep in John 10: 16. These are the ten northern tribes that will one day be brought back together with the two southern tribes (cf. Ezek 37:16ff).
- The Lord tells the unbelieving Jews, "[25] Jesus answered them, 'I told you, and ye believed not: the works that I do in my Father's name, they bear witness of me. [26] But ye believe not, because ye are not of my sheep, as I said unto you. [27] My sheep hear my voice, and I know them, and they follow me: [28] And I give unto them eternal life; and they shall never perish, neither shall any *man* pluck them out of my hand.'" (John 10:25-28)
- Those who receive eternal life in Verse 28 are those who hear His voice in Verse 27. To be a disciple in John 10, they had to "continue in my words…" as in John 8:31 "If ye continue in my word then are ye my disciples indeed."

The Hebrews in 5:12-14 are those that will have to go on to perfection (Heb. 6:1) if they are to get into the Kingdom of Heaven. However, Israel's current state during this present dispensation of grace is stated in Romans 9:31-33. They followed after the law of righteousness and have therefore not attained to the law of righteousness because they sought it not by faith.

Study Guides Questions on Chapter 5

1. Summarize five of the characteristics of the High Priests that are taken from among men.
2. Who, according to Verses 4 and 5, called Christ to be a High Priest? When was he called?
3. What was Jesus concerned about in His strong prayers? What saves from death?
4. In what sense did Christ have to be made perfect in Verse 9?
5. Of what order is Christ's Priesthood in Verse 10?
6. What is it about the Hebrews in Verses 11 – 14 that concerns the writer?

CHAPTER 6
GOING ON THE PERFECTION

Hebrews 6: 1-3 "Therefore leaving the principles of the doctrine of Christ, let us go on unto perfection; not laying again the foundation of repentance from dead works, and of faith toward God, ²Of the doctrine of baptisms, and of laying on of hands, and of resurrection of the dead, and of eternal judgment. ³ And this will we do, if God permit."

"Therefore, ..." in verse 1 goes back to 5:12-14 where the Hebrews had need that one teach them again which are the first principles of the oracles of God. Now, having gone through those first principles again in chapters 1 through 5, the writer goes "...on to perfection." The perfection is that referred to in 2:18 and 5:9. It is the doctrine that Christ was made perfect as the High Priest after the order of Melchisedec. That is the doctrine that will take them on to perfection. He accomplished this by the sacrifice of His perfect life on the cross and the bringing in of the New Covenant to replace the Old Covenant. The Old Covenant "...made nothing perfect." (Heb 7:19) The "first principles of the oracles of God..." are the things the Lord taught them in Matthew, Mark, Luke and John.

Note in Luke 9:43-45 and 18:33-34 the Lord tells them of His death but the apostles rebuke Him. They did not understand what He said and the saying was hid from them. In Luke 24:44 the Lord tells them "⁴⁴ ... These *are* the words which I spake unto you, while I was yet with you, that all things must be fulfilled, which were written in the law of Moses, and *in* the prophets, and *in* the psalms, concerning me."

The four Gospels do not contain an exposé of what was accomplished by the cross. It is the book of Romans that presents an expository explanation of the cross to us Gentiles in the Dispensation of Grace. It is then the book of Hebrews that takes the doctrine of Romans Chapter 3 that presents the cross as the means of redemption to the Hebrew people. In John 16:12-13, the Lord tells them: "¹² I have yet many things to say unto you, but ye cannot bear them now. ¹³ Howbeit when he, the Spirit of truth, is come, he will guide you into all truth: for he shall not speak of himself; but whatsoever he shall hear, *that* shall he speak: and he will shew you things to come." Hebrews 6:1 and following tells the Hebrew people those things to come. God is using the same mode of revelation to reveal the merits of the cross to the Hebrews that He used to reveal the Mystery to us (Eph. 3:1; Gal. 1:16, 2:9).

The writer of Hebrews urges his readers "...Let us go on to perfection..." This means that perfection was not there yet in the doctrine presented in the four Gospels or even in the Book of Acts. The disciples and the little flock were still under the Law of Moses (Matt. 23:2-3) and "the Law made nothing perfect" (Heb. 7:19).What was still missing for the Hebrew people was an understanding of what really was accomplished by the cross (Luke 9:43-45, 18: 33-34, 24:34-49). The Lord tells the disciples "I have yet many things to say unto you, but ye cannot bear them now. Howbeit when he, the Spirit of truth, is come, he will guide you into all truth: for he shall not speak of himself; but whatsoever he shall hear, that shall he speak: and he will show you things to come." (John 16:12-13).

"...Not laying again the foundation of repentance from dead works..." Dead works are defined for the Hebrews as their "...vain conversation received by tradition from your fathers." (1Peter 1:18, cf. Matt. 3:5-12 and Lev. 26:38-42). The repentance in view here is the baptism of repentance that John the Baptist called Israel to in Matthew 3:1-5. Note Matthew 3:5-6: "⁵ Then went out to him Jerusalem, and all Judaea, and all the region round about Jordan, ⁶ And were baptized of him in Jordan, confessing their sins." This confessing of sins is the repentance referred to in Leviticus 26:38-40. This repentance would get Israel out from under the five successive courses of judgment of

Leviticus 26. Note that this repentance is "from dead works." Dead works are works that can not produce life. To repent of them is to leave those dead works behind.

"...Faith toward God..." is what Christ's earthly ministry was to accomplish in Israel (John 5:12, 24). "²⁸ Then said they unto him, What shall we do, that we might work the works of God? ²⁹ Jesus answered and said unto them, This is the work of God, that ye believe on him whom he hath sent." (John 6:28-29)

"The doctrine of baptisms..." relates to what John the Baptist had taught regarding the three baptisms of Matthew 3:11-12, the death baptism that the Lord spoke of in Luke 12:50; the commission baptism of Matthew 28:19 and Spirit baptism of Acts 1:5. These verses list six of the twelve baptisms referred to in scripture. All six of these pertain to Israel and the prophetic program. The one baptism that pertains to us today (Ephesians 4:5; 1Corinthians 12:12-13; Galatians 3:27; Romans 6:1-6; Colossians 2:12; etc.) involves the work of the Holy Spirit to form the Body of Christ.

"The laying on of hands..." is a reference to the healing ministry that accompanied the proclamation of the Gospel of the Kingdom (Mark 16:18).

"The resurrection of the dead..." must be distinguished from the resurrection from the dead. Christ was raised from the dead (Mark 9:9-10, 31). There will be a resurrection "of the dead" in the future (Matt. 22:31, Luke 20:37-38). Resurrection life (as we saw earlier) is the basic promise of the Abrahamic Covenant.

Eternal judgment is a reference to the Lord's teaching in Matthew 25:31-46. This judgment is based on the covenant that God made with Abraham in which God would bless them that bless Abraham and his seed and curse them that cursed his seed.

"If God permit..." is actually a part of the warning that follows. If the Lord returns before they go on to perfection, they will not get into the kingdom. To go on to perfection for an Israelite who had gone through the earthly teaching ministry of our Lord would be to go on to putting one's trust in the shed blood of Christ. This is what the remainder of the book of Hebrews will present to them. The "...if God permits..." is meant to point out that if the Lord returns before they go on to perfection in this regard, they would not get into the kingdom. Peter warns Israel that the Lord will come "...as a thief in the night." (2Peter 3:10) and some could end up being caught off guard. If the Lord were to return before they went on to perfection, then God did not permit them to go on to perfection. Not because He did not want them to (2Peter 3:9) but because they did not heed the warning to go on to perfection.

> Hebrews 6 4-6 "⁴For *it is* impossible for those who were once enlightened, and have tasted of the heavenly gift, and were made partakers of the Holy Ghost, ⁵ And have tasted the good word of God, and the powers of the world to come, ⁶ If they shall fall away, to renew them again unto repentance; seeing they crucify to themselves the Son of God afresh, and put *him* to an open shame."

The Third Warning (Hebrews 5:11 – 6:20) -- Don't be dull of hearing but be mature in your understanding.

"It is impossible..." This is a warning to the Hebrews of what will happen if they do not go on to perfection. This is part of their program whereby they had to endure to the end (Matt. 10:21-24) to get into the Kingdom. Israel's situation in early Acts and in the coming Tribulation is a replay of what they faced in Numbers 13 and 14 at Kadesh where they failed to enter the land for fear of the giants. They failed for unbelief – not believing that God would deliver the giants into their hands. Acts 2:39-42 equates to Numbers 13 in that some believed (Acts 2:45-47) while others (the majority) did not. To understand where the Hebrew people are in their God-ordained program in regard to the establishment of the promised Kingdom, we need to consider the seven feasts in which Israel lived out their prophetic future each year (Lev. 23:5-28). Each of these seven feasts were types of sequential steps in God's program of redemption for Israel. Let's look at the feasts and consider the fulfillment of each:

The Seven Feasts of the LORD in Leviticus 23

1. Passover – The first Passover was in Egypt (Ex. 13:6). The real Passover was the cross for it was there that the blood that allows God to pass over judgment on Israel's sins (and ours) was shed (1Cor. 5:7).

2. Unleavened Bread – Leaven is a type of sin. What was accomplished on Calvary was the putting away of sin. (Luke 22:7).

3. The **Feast of First Fruits** marked the beginning of the harvest. The real harvest in view here though is the harvest of souls from the dead. Christ is the First Fruits of them that slept (1Cor. 15:20) and the First Begotten from the dead (Rev. 1:5).

4. Pentecost is the empowering of Israel with the Holy Ghost to be the means of bringing in New Covenant and the Kingdom. Israel's program was temporarily interrupted by the stoning of Stephen in Acts 7. The stoning of Stephen was a crisis point in Israel's history. Stephen was the unwilling messenger that Israel sent to God saying in effect "we will not have this man [Christ] to reign over us..." (Luke 19:4).

These four (as to their antitypes) have been fulfilled. There is a long delay between the fourth feast (Pentecost) and the fifth (Trumpets) in Israel's annual calendar. Likewise, there will be a long delay in the fulfillment of the next step in Israel's plan of redemption. What is next on God's redemptive program for Israel is the re-gathering of the nation from among the Gentiles and Israel's real Day of Atonement. We today in the Dispensation of Grace received the atonement the instant that we trusted Jesus Christ as Savior (Rom. 5:11). However, Israel still looks forward to her real Day of Atonement. Peter speaks of that day in Acts 3:19 when he told Israel, "Repent ye therefore, and be converted, that your sins may be blotted out when the times of refreshing shall come from the presence of the Lord..." This will be the fulfillment of the Feast of Trumpets. Ezekiel 20:34-36 speaks of this fulfillment. The book of Hebrews is preparing Israel for this next step in their program.

5. Trumpets will herald Israel's re-gathering. That will be the next step in their program. This will happen at the close of the Tribulation Period.

6. Atonement Israel's **Day of Atonement** will come after the close of the Tribulation Period. (Heb. 10:16-17). Israel's Day of Atonement will come "from the presence of the Lord." (Acts 3:19). Peter said in Acts 15:11 "11 But we [Jews] believe that through the grace of the Lord Jesus Christ we shall [in the future] be saved, even as they [as they (the Gentiles) are being saved today]. Believers today in the Dispensation of Grace "have received the atonement." (Rom. 5:11). Israel still waits for her Day of Atonement.

7. Tabernacles The real fulfillment of the **Feast of Tabernacles** will come when "...the tabernacle of God is with men, and he will dwell with them, and they shall be his people and God himself, shall be with them, and be their God. (Rev. 21:4). The book of Hebrews looks forward to that day (Heb. 8:11).

"...For those who were once enlightened..." We note that everything in Hebrews 6:3-5 is in the past tense:
- They were once enlightened...
- They tasted of the heavenly gift...
- They were made partakers of the Holy Ghost...
- They tasted the good word of God...
- They tasted of the powers of the world to come.

All of these things happened to the Hebrew believers in Acts Chapters 2 thru 5. The salvation that is in view in the book of Hebrews is a salvation that requires one to "endure to the end..." (Matt.10:22). It is not a salvation that is offered as a free gift of God's grace as it is today in the Dispensation of Grace. We today are saved (Eph. 2:8-10), justified (Rom. 3:22-26), sealed (Eph. 1:13), and we have already received the atonement (Rom 5:11) the instant that we trust Jesus Christ as Savior. These Hebrews had to go on to perfection. The perfection that they had to go on to was faith in the shed blood of Christ. The doctrine of the blood atonement in the context of Israel's program is presented in the upcoming chapters of Hebrews.

This again relates back to the experience of the twelve spies of Numbers 13. All of the spies tasted of the wealth of the land but ten of them did not enter the land because of unbelief. The actual offer of the Kingdom of Heaven to Israel was in Acts Chapter 2 (Acts 2:39-42).

It should also be noted that the Hebrew people who were reading this epistle were not (at the time of the reading of it) tasting of the heavenly gift nor were they tasting of the powers of the world to come. They were not all that "enlightened" anymore either (Heb. 5:11 cf. Acts 28:27). The reason for their lack of experiencing these things is that their program was interrupted by the present Dispensation of Grace.

If they shall fall away... Israel, at this point in their program, did not have absolute security as we have (see Ephesians 1:12-13 whereby we are sealed unto the day of redemption). The stoning of Stephen was Israel's answer to the offer of the kingdom. Stephen was the messenger in the Lord's parable in Luke 19:14. Though Israel's program was interrupted, Jesus Christ is nonetheless Israel's High Priest who is today within the veil (Heb. 6:17-20) as the guarantor of Israel's future hope. For those who go on in their understanding to trust Him, He will appear again "without sin unto salvation." (Heb. 9:28).

For *it is* impossible ... to renew them again unto repentance... Israel had been in repentance under the ministry of John (Matt 3:2) and at Pentecost (Act 2:38). The believers of Israel will go on to perfection during the coming Tribulation Period. As we saw earlier, this will be a replay of the wilderness experience. "[36] Like as I pleaded with your fathers in the wilderness of the land of Egypt, so will I plead with you, saith the Lord GOD. [37] And I will cause you to pass under the rod, and I will bring you into the bond of the covenant: [38] And I will purge out from among you the rebels, and them that transgress against me: I will bring them forth out of the country where they sojourn, and they shall not enter into the land of Israel: and ye shall know that I *am* the LORD." (Ezek 20:36-38)

Verse 6 says of them that they "crucify to themselves the Son of God afresh..." To go back to the Law of Moses with the animal sacrifices would be to say in effect that the cross accomplished nothing and thus put Him to open shame. They would crucify to themselves the Son of God afresh in that the animal sacrifices were a type of the crucifixion of Christ.

Hebrews 6: 7-12 "For the earth which drinketh in the rain that cometh oft upon it, and bringeth forth herbs meet for them by whom it is dressed, receiveth blessing from God: [8] But that which beareth thorns and briers *is* rejected, and *is* nigh unto cursing; whose end *is* to be burned. [9] But, beloved, we are persuaded better things of you, and things that accompany salvation, though we thus speak. [10] For God *is* not unrighteous to forget your work and labour of love, which ye have shewed toward his name, in that ye have ministered to the saints, and do minister. [11] And we desire that every one of you do shew the same diligence to the full assurance of hope unto the end: [12] That ye be not slothful, but followers of them who through faith and patience inherit the promises."

Believers here are likened to good earth. Earth that brings forth briers is cursed. Israel is likened to a vineyard. "The vineyard of the LORD of hosts is the house of Israel, and the men of Judah his pleasant plant: and he looked for judgment but behold oppression, for righteousness but behold a cry." (Isa. 5:1-7). An Israelite can only bear the kind of fruit that the Lord is looking for by abiding in Christ (John 15:6). Christ is the True Vine (the true Israel) and the Hebrews are the branches.

Here in Verse 8 and 9 we see labor and work associated with salvation. Our justification today in the Dispensation of Grace is apart from works (Rom. 4:2, 5; Gal. 2:16) while in Israel's program works are involved in justification (James 2:21-22). These Hebrews had to be followers of them who "...through faith and patience inherit the promise." We will see this again in Hebrews 10:32-36.

Hebrews 6: 13-19 "[13]For when God made promise to Abraham, because he could swear by no greater, he sware by himself, [14] Saying, Surely blessing I will bless thee, and multiplying I will multiply thee. [15] And so, after he had patiently endured, he obtained the promise. [16] For men verily swear by the greater: and an oath for confirmation *is* to them an end of all strife. [17] Wherein God, willing more abundantly to shew unto the heirs of promise the immutability of his counsel, confirmed *it* by an oath: [18] That by two immutable things, in which *it was* impossible for God to lie, we might have a strong consolation, who have fled for refuge to lay hold upon the hope set before us: [19] Which *hope* we have as an anchor of the soul, both sure and stedfast, and which entereth into that within the veil; [20] Whither the forerunner is for us entered, *even* Jesus, made an high priest for ever after the order of Melchisedec."

There are two immutable assurances of the promise that God made to Abraham and to his seed. The first is that God could swear by none greater than Himself and so He did that – He made an oath with Himself that the promises of the Abrahamic covenant are sure to all the seed of Abraham. The second is that God can not lie.

Israel's Cities of Refuge

Verse 18 speaks of fleeing for refuge. This causes us to think of the cities of refuge that God had established in Israel. Numbers 35 gives us information on these cities of refuge. There were six such cities of refuge scattered around Israel. If someone killed someone by accident, that person could flee to one of these cities and find refuge from "the avenger of blood" until that person could get a fair trial by the congregation. A murderer was to be put to death by the avenger of blood (Numbers 35:18-19). However, if the man killed by accident and the congregation so judged, he may flee to a city of refuge and abide there until the death of the high priest. If the man leaves the city of refuge before the death of the high priest, the avenger of blood may kill him and not be guilty of murder. After the death of the high priest, the man may safely return to his home and his possession. This all sounds like a very strange policy. However, if we see these cities of refuge being types of Christ, this whole thing starts to get real interesting. Israel was guilty of murdering her Messiah. However, on the cross, the Lord changed the charge from murder to man slaughter (second degree murder) when He said "Father, forgive them for they know not what they do." (Luke 23:34). Therefore, if Christ be the refuge, only those who are in Christ will escape the avenger of blood. They have to stay in Christ (the refuge) until the death of the high priest. If the high priest will live forever, their eternal life is dependent on them staying in Christ. The avenger of blood (who turns out to be the antichrist) will (during the coming Tribulation Period) kill those who are not in Christ the Refuge. God thus purges Israel of unbelief "...And so all Israel shall be saved" (Rom. 11:26). This does get interesting!

Study Guides Questions on Chapter 6

1. What basic doctrines is the writer of Hebrews leaving behind as he goes on to perfection with them?
2. Where in the Bible do we find the basic doctrines that they will need to leave and move on from?
3. What important information is not addressed in Matthew, Mark, Luke and John?
4. What would be the foundation of repentance from dead works in Verse 11?
5. To what baptisms does Verse 2 refer?
6. Is resurrection of the dead the same as resurrection from the dead?
7. What eternal judgment is in view in Verse 2?
8. What does Verse 3 mean saying "If God permit" regarding going on the perfection?
9. Why would it be impossible to renew these that fall away again unto repentance?
10. Who were those who were once enlightened?
11. In what sense would labor and work be associated with salvation in Verses 8 & 9?
12. What are the two immutable things in Verse 18?

CHAPTER 7
A PRIEST AFTER THE ORDER OF MELCHISEDEC

An Overview of Chapters 7 through 10

Chapter 7 will go into the details of the priesthood that is "after the order of Melchisedec." This is a new and better order of priesthood than the priesthood of the Old Testament. Chapters 8 to 10 will then provide details on how the ministry of that priesthood is better than that of the Old Covenant priesthood (the priesthood after the order of Aaron). The doctrinal theme of Hebrews is this new priesthood ministered to Israel by the Lord Jesus Christ. The book is addressed to two groups of Hebrews. First it is addressed to those who came through the earthly ministry of Christ but now needed to go on in faith to this added information. That is to say that they needed to go on to perfection as Hebrews 6:1-4 admonished them to do. Secondly, it will be addressed particularly to the future Hebrews who will go through the coming Tribulation Period. Hebrews 5:1-10 introduced the fact that Jesus Christ is to be a high priest after the order of Melchisedec but gives us no real details. Then in Hebrews 5:11-6:20 we see a warning to the hearers to actually hear the doctrine in the coming chapters (see notes on 5:11). In Hebrews 6:19 we see that Christ went in within the veil. This is what the priests after the order of Aaron did on Israel's Day of Atonement each year. Let's consider what happened annually on that day under the Aaronic priesthood as described in Leviticus 16.

- Two goats were taken. One was killed, and the other (the scapegoat) was sent out into the wilderness.
- A ram was killed for a burnt offering.
- A bullock was offered for Aaron and his family to make atonement for himself.
- The high priest goes in behind the veil. However, the atonement is not complete until he comes back out.

The anti type of Leviticus 16 is here in Hebrews. Jesus Christ went behind the veil in heaven and has not come back out yet. He went behind the veil for Israel as her High Priest – a priest after the order of Melchisedec. He is still to this day there. He is there as the head of the church the body of Christ to represent us who live in the dispensation of grace. He is also there as Israel's High Priest to provide the assurance that Israel still has a future in God's plan for the ages.

Hebrews 7

> **Hebrews 7:1-3** "For this Melchisedec, king of Salem, priest of the most high God, who met Abraham returning from the slaughter of the kings, and blessed him; [2] To whom also Abraham gave a tenth part of all; first being by interpretation King of righteousness, and after that also King of Salem, which is, King of peace; [3] Without father, without mother, without descent, having neither beginning of days, nor end of life; but made like unto the Son of God; abideth a priest continually."

So who is Melchisedec? The Old Testament account of the event that the writer is referring to is in Genesis 14:18-20. The next and only other mention of him is in Psalm 110:1-4 in connection with the prophecy of Christ sitting at the Father's right hand until His enemies are made His footstool. But while He is there He is "a priest forever after the order of Melchisedec." Note that it is not "of the order of Melchisedec..." but "after the order..." Christ is not in the lineage of the priesthood of Melchisedec but His priesthood is similar in type to that of Melchisedec. With that in mind, let's consider who the Melchisedec of Genesis was:

- We know that he was a man (Heb. 7:4).
- His name means "King of Righteousness."
- He was the king of Salem (Salem means Peace).
- He was "the priest of the most high God." (Gen. 14:2)
- He blessed Abraham. (Heb. 7:7)
- He lived before Levi (the priestly tribe in Israel).
- Abraham gave tithes to Melchisedec.
- His priesthood has no recorded genealogy (no beginning of days as a priest or end of his tour of duty).

Salem (Jerusalem) was in the hands of the Jebusites in Joshua 12:10. David finally conquered Jerusalem in 2 Samuel 5:5-7. Note in Zechariah 6:12-13 that Christ will be both a priest and a king. "...Behold the man whose name is The BRANCH; and he shall grow up out of his place, and he shall build the temple of the LORD...and shall sit and rule upon his throne; and he shall be a priest upon his throne: and the counsel of peace shall be between them both." (Zech. 6:12-13) Jeremiah 23:5-6 again teaches this "Behold, the days come, saith the LORD, that I will raise unto David a righteous Branch, and a King shall reign and prosper, and shall execute judgment and justice in the earth. In his days Judah shall be saved, and Israel shall dwell safely: and this is his name whereby he shall be called, THE LORD OUR RIGHTEOUSNESS." (Jer. 23:5-6)

As an interesting side note: there are four "branch" titles found in scriptures in reference to the Lord. There is an interesting correspondence between them and the four Gospel records:

1. The Branch of the LORD (Isa. 4:2). This compares to John's Gospel which presents Christ as God in human flesh.
2. The Branch out of Jesse (Isa. 11:1) This compares to Matthew's Gospel which presents Christ as the King (Jer. 23:5-6,33:15)
3. My Servant the Branch (Zech. 3:8). This compares to Mark's Gospel which presents Christ as the Servant (Isa. 52:13-15, 53:1-12; Phil. 2:5-8).
4. The Man whose name is "The Branch" (Zech. 6:12-13). This compares to Luke's Gospel which presents Christ as the perfect man.

Melchisedec was king of Salem – Jerusalem.

> "The LORD hath sworn in truth unto David; he will not turn from it; Of the fruit of thy body will I set upon thy throne. If thy children will keep my covenant and my testimony that I shall teach them, their children shall also sit upon thy throne for evermore. For the LORD hath chosen Zion; he hath desired it for his habitation." (Psalm 132:11-13)

Zion is Jerusalem. David conquered it from the Jebusites and it became the city of David (1Kings 8:1). The name "Jerusalem" is equivalent to Zion (2Kings 19:31) though the name Zion is more specifically the temple site (1Chr. 11:7). "In Salem also is his tabernacle, and his dwelling place in Zion." (Psalm 76:2). Luke 21:24 says that Jerusalem shall be trodden under foot of the Gentiles until the kingdom is established. However, one day "...out of Zion shall go forth the law, and the word of the LORD from Jerusalem." (Isa. 2:2-3).

Verse 2 speaks of Melchisedec as "...First being by interpretation King of righteousness, and after that also King of Salem, which is, King of peace..." J. Vernon McGee says of the name Melchizedek: "Melchizedek was also the 'King of righteousness.' That is what the name Melchizedek means: melek is a Hebrew word meaning 'king,' and tsedeq means 'righteousness.' Jeremiah speaks of Jehovah-tsidkenu, meaning 'Jehovah our righteousness.'" (*Thru The Bible* with J. Vernon McGee). This man's name was "King of Righteousness" but he was also the king of Salem meaning Peace. This man is a type of Christ. Before Christ could be the King of Peace, He had to be the King of Righteousness. Isaiah 32:17 says it well: "And the work of righteousness shall be peace; and the effect of righteousness quietness and assurance for ever." The angel that announced His birth said: "...Glory to God in the highest, and on earth peace, good will toward men."(Luke 2:14). The reason that there is no real peace on earth today is that there is no proper glory given to God nor is there true righteousness.

Verse 3 requires careful thought: "Without father, without mother, without descent, having neither beginning of days, nor end of life..." Melchizedek is here said to be:

- Without father
- Without mother
- Without descent
- Having neither beginning of days
- Nor end of life
- But made like unto the Son of God.

So the question is: "Who was he?" All that we can know of him is what the scripture says of him. The most obvious fact we get is that he was a man (Heb. 7:4). Therefore, the statement "without father, without mother..." can not be a reference to his physical person. All men (except Adam and Christ) had both a physical father and mother. He was not Adam. Also, he was not a pre-incarnate Christ because Christ had a physical mother. The best way to understand this is to note that the whole passage has to deal with Melchizedek's priesthood. Note that Verse 3 says that he was made "...like unto the Son of God." It does not say that he was "made the Son of God." There is a similitude of Melchizedek and Christ in their respective priesthoods. According to Scripture, Melchizedek was a priest appointed by God to a position that had neither a defined beginning of days nor and end of operation of the office. His having neither beginning of days nor end of life has to do with his genealogy as a priest. This was not the case with the priesthood of Aaron. The priests of the tribe of Levi were to start their priestly duties at age 25 and retire from that position at age 50 (Num. 8:24-26). The priests after the order of Aaron had a beginning of days to their service and an end of life to their priesthood.

> **Hebrews 7:4-10** "Now consider how great this man *was*, unto whom even the patriarch Abraham gave the tenth of the spoils. [5] And verily they that are of the sons of Levi, who receive the office of the priesthood, have a commandment to take tithes of the people according to the law, that is, of their brethren, though they come out of the loins of Abraham: [6] But he whose descent is not counted from them received tithes of Abraham, and blessed him that had the promises. [7] And without all contradiction the less is blessed of the better. [8] And here men that die receive tithes; but there he *receiveth them*, of whom it is witnessed that he liveth. [9] And as I may so say, Levi also, who receiveth tithes, payed tithes in Abraham. [10] For he was yet in the loins of his father, when Melchisedec met him."

Verse 4 brings the issue of the tithe into focus: "...Unto whom...Abraham gave the tenth..." Abraham gave a tenth of the spoils from his victory over the kings in Genesis 14 to Melchisedec. Abraham understood that it was God who gave him the victory and therefore recognized this by giving a tithe to God's priest. Abraham recognized Melchisedec's priesthood. There are only three verses that give the history of the event in Genesis (Gen. 14:18-20).

There we see that Melchisedec brought bread and wine to Abraham after the victory and said "Blessed be Abraham of the most high God, possessor of heaven and earth: And blessed be the most high God, which hath delivered thine enemies into thy hand..." (Gen. 14:19-20). Bread and wine are things that bless men: "...wine ...maketh glad the heart of man ... and bread which strengtheneth man's heart..." (Psalm 104:15; Eccl. 9:7). Today, we have a memorial of the blessing that we have in Christ that involves bread and wine (1Cor. 10:16; 11:26 cf Luke 22:20; Matt. 26:26-29).

Verses 4 through 9 are still addressing the superiority of the priesthood of Melchizedek over that of the descendents of Aaron. Two points are made to stress this:

The sons of Levi who receive tithes according to the Law actually paid tithes in Abraham to Melchizedek
Abraham (the father of Levi) was blessed by Melchizedek and "...without all contradiction the less is blessed of the better."

Hebrews 7:11-14 "If therefore perfection were by the Levitical priesthood, (for under it the people received the law,) what further need *was there* that another priest should rise after the order of Melchisedec, and not be called after the order of Aaron? 12 For the priesthood being changed, there is made of necessity a change also of the law. 13 For he of whom these things are spoken pertaineth to another tribe, of which no man gave attendance at the altar. 14 For *it is* evident that our Lord sprang out of Juda; of which tribe Moses spake nothing concerning priesthood."

Note that the issue in verse 11 is still perfection. The point is that if the Levitical priesthood could have brought in perfection, there would be no further need for another priest after the order of Melchizedek. The Old Covenant of the Law had a priesthood, but that covenant was giving way to a new covenant (Jer. 31:31). The New Covenant is going to last forever. Therefore, the priesthood of the New Covenant would also have to be everlasting (Jer. 32:40, Ezek. 37:26).

Hebrews 7: 15-25 "And it is yet far more evident: for that after the similitude of Melchisedec there ariseth another priest, 16 Who is made, not after the law of a carnal commandment, but after the power of an endless life. 17 For he testifieth, Thou *art* a priest for ever after the order of Melchisedec. 18 For there is verily a disannulling of the commandment going before for the weakness and unprofitableness thereof. 19 For the law made nothing perfect, but the bringing in of a better hope *did*; by the which we draw nigh unto God. 20 And inasmuch as not without an oath *he was made priest*: 21 (For those priests were made without an oath; but this with an oath by him that said unto him, The Lord sware and will not repent, Thou *art* a priest for ever after the order of Melchisedec. 22 By so much was Jesus made a surety of a better testament. 23 And they truly were many priests, because they were not suffered to continue by reason of death: 24 But this *man*, because he continueth ever, hath an unchangeable priesthood. 25 Wherefore he is able also to save them to the uttermost that come unto God by him, seeing he ever liveth to make intercession for them."

In Psalm 110:4 Christ (who comes from the tribe of Judah) is declared to be a priest forever but not after a commandment given to men but according to the power of a resurrection to eternal life (that is – the power of an endless life). Christ could not be a priest under the Old Covenant. Therefore, there had to be a New Covenant. God does not do away with the Law (Jer. 31: 33-34) but He does away with the Old Covenant. He does this by giving them a New Covenant by which He gives them righteousness. Unlike the Levitical priesthood, the priesthood of Christ is made with an oath (Psalm 110:4).

Malachi 3:3 says of the Messiah "And he shall sit as a refiner and purifier of silver: and he shall purify the sons of Levi, and purge them as gold and silver, that they may offer unto the LORD an offering in righteousness." In Numbers Chapter 25 Verses 11 through 13 we see that Phinehas, the son of Eleazar, the son of Aaron the priest was to have "...the covenant of an everlasting priesthood." That would imply that Phinehas' decedents would be priests in the kingdom. It appears then that the Levitical priesthood will still operate in the kingdom (Mal. 3:3 cf Num. 25:13) along with the high priesthood of Christ. These sacrifices offered by them would be only a memorial (probably much like our communion). However, the real sacrifice that accomplishes redemption is that made of the Lord Jesus Christ as the high priest of Israel.

> **Hebrews 7: 26-28** "For such an high priest became us, *who is* holy, harmless, undefiled, separate from sinners, and made higher than the heavens; [27] Who needeth not daily, as those high priests, to offer up sacrifice, first for his own sins, and then for the people's: for this he did once, when he offered up himself. [28] For the law maketh men high priests which have infirmity; but the word of the oath, which was since the law, *maketh* the Son, who is consecrated for evermore."

Verses 24-25 says because He ever liveth, "... he is able also to save them to the uttermost..." Such a high priest (one who lives forever to make intercession for us) became us. That is, He became a man and entered into our humanity. The Lord Jesus Christ did not have to do what the high priests of the Aaronic priesthood did – offer up sacrifices first for their own sins before they could offer sacrifices for the people. Christ could offer one sacrifice (that of His own perfect life) once because He had no sin Himself and could therefore offer one sacrifice that settled the account of Israel's sin once for all – and that of our sins as well.

The Law made without an oath appointed priests who had human infirmities. The oath of Psalm 110:1-4 however was after the Law and supplanted the Law to appoint and consecrate Christ as a priest forever who did not have infirmities.

From Hebrews 7:19 onward, the book of Hebrews lists seven "better things" that the New Covenant brings:

1. A Better Hope (7:19) – deliverance from sin
2. A Better Testament (7:22) – one based on grace and forgiveness
3. A Better Promise (8:6) – the promise of righteousness
4. A Better Sacrifice (9:23) – a divine sacrifice
5. A Better Substance (10:34) – one that endures
6. A Better Country (11:16) – a heavenly country set up on earth
7. A Better Resurrection (11:35) – as a result of faithfulness.

Study Guides Questions on Chapter 7

1. What are four things that Old Testament priests did on their annual Day of Atonement?
2. What are the antitypes of those things done by Israel's High Priest?
3. What do we know about Melchisedec by comparing Hebrews Chapter 7 with Genesis 14:18-25? List eight things.
4. What does verse 3 mean regarding Melchisedec being without father or mother?
5. What two things are seen changing in verse 12?
6. Does God do away with the Law or is it the Old Covenant that He does away with?
7. What does verse 26 mean saying "such a high priest became us?"
8. Why did the High Priest of the Old Testament offer two sacrifices while Christ offered only one? What were those two sacrifices? What was the one sacrifice that He offered?
9. What oath does verse 28 refer to? Was there an oath for the priest after the order of Aaron?

AN OVERVIEW OF HEBREWS CHAPTERS 8 THROUGH 10

Having introduced the concept of Jesus Christ as being Israel's High Priest after a new order (in the similitude of the order of Melchisedec), the Book of Hebrews proceeds to answer some important questions on His (Christ's) office of high priest. The questions are:

1. Why does Israel need a high priest?
2. What exactly is the office of the high priest?
3. How can Christ be a high priest being not from the tribe of Levi?
4. What does the Lord Jesus Christ do for Israel as her High Priest?
5. What is Israel's relationship to Christ in His capacity as the high priest?

These are the questions. Now for the answers:

1. Why does Israel need a high priest? Israel needs a high priest to represent the nation before God and to guarantee her future. He is the means whereby Israel can get through the coming Tribulation Period, to "obtain mercy, and find grace to help in time of need." (Heb. 4:16).

2. What does it mean to be a high priest? The high priest made atonement for the sins of the nation. The high priest after the order of Aaron went into the Holy of Holies on earth once a year with the atoning blood sacrifice and then came out to release the sins of the people on the scapegoat. So too Christ, after a new order of priesthood (that of Melchisedec), went into the real Holy of Holies in Heaven with his own blood to make atonement for their sins. We saw this in Hebrews 5:6 and we will see it again in Hebrews 9:5-12.

3. How can Christ be Israel's high priest when He is not from the tribe of Levi? He can be a high priest because He was called of God to be a high priest as was Melchisedec. The Lord Jesus Christ is a priest forever after the order of Melchisedec. Note that it is *after* the order of Melchisedec – not *of* the order of Melchisedec. His priesthood was not after that of Aaron's and the Old Covenant but after (in similitude to) that of Melchisedec. A new order of priesthood was needed because there was to be a change of the Covenant. "[12] For the priesthood being changed, there is made of necessity a change also of the law. For he of whom these things are spoken pertaineth to another tribe, of which no man gave attendance at the altar. For *it is* evident that our Lord sprang out of Juda; of which tribe Moses spake nothing concerning priesthood. And it is yet far more evident: for that after the similitude of Melchisedec there ariseth another priest, Who is made, not after the law of a carnal commandment, but after the power of an endless life." (Heb. 7:12-16). The Old Covenant could not bring the promised blessing to Israel, so a new covenant is needed. Just as the Old Covenant had a priesthood, so also does the New Covenant. Jesus Christ is the High Priest of the New Covenant.

4. What does Christ do for them as the high priest? Christ pleads for the nation as Moses did. Hebrews was written after the fall of Israel to explain their status before God in light of the dispensational change that took place. The books of Hebrews through the Revelation will have their application for Israel after the close of the dispensation of grace to give Israel the information that they will need to get through the tribulation and into the Kingdom. An Israelite who trusts Jesus Christ as Savior today in the dispensation of grace becomes a member of the church which is Christ's body. After this dispensation closes, Israel will again need the High Priestly work of Jesus Christ. Israel's motivation to endure through the coming Great Tribulation Period is going to be in Christ's priestly work.

"So Christ was once offered to bear the sins of many; and unto them that look for him shall he appear the second time without sin unto salvation." (Heb. 9:28) Under the Old Covenant, sins were covered by the blood of animal sacrifices one year at a time. However, "...it is not possible that the blood of bulls and goats should take away sins." (Heb. 10:4). Therefore, Jesus Christ as Israel's High Priest after a new order puts away sins by the sacrifice of Himself to obtain for them eternal salvation.

5. What is Israel's relationship to her High Priest? The Lord Jesus Christ is today behind the veil where "...He is able also to save them to the uttermost that come unto God by him, seeing he ever liveth to make intercession for them." (Heb. 7:25). Israel's real Day of Atonement is yet in the future from where we are at in history today in the dispensation of grace. To understand this we need to go back to Leviticus 16:15ff and understand the type of the Day of Atonement that was lived out annually in the Old Covenant.

On Israel's annual Day of Atonement:
- Two goats were selected.
- One was sacrificed by the shedding of its blood.
- The High Priest went in to the Holy of Holies behind the veil with its blood and put it on the altar.
- The High Priest then comes out from behind the veil.
- The sins of the nation are put upon the other goat (the scapegoat) and the scapegoat is sent away into the wilderness never to be seen again.
- Jesus Christ is today behind the veil in Heaven as the guarantor of Israel's future. One day He will come out from behind the veil and bring Israel's real Day of Atonement when He comes to the nation after defeating Israel's enemies at Armageddon.

The veil of the Old Covenant tabernacle was a type of Heaven. The Old Testament high priest went behind the veil once each year. It must be remembered that what Aaron did once per year he did behind the veil. "But Christ being come an high priest of good things to come, by a greater and more perfect tabernacle, not made with hands, that is to say, not of this building; 12 Neither by the blood of goats and calves, but by his own blood he entered in once into the holy place, having obtained eternal redemption *for us*." (Hebrews 9:11-12) What Christ does as high priest He does behind the veil (in heaven). He went in once for all time because He obtained eternal redemption for the believing remnant of Israel. He went in not with the blood of goats but with His own blood. His work did more than make atonement for sin for a year but rather for all time and redeemed them from dead works in the process. His work behind the veil enabled Him to become the mediator of the New Covenant for Israel. He will one day come out from behind the veil and will appear again a second time without sin unto salvation (sin had been dealt with at Calvary and it will not be an issue anymore).

Israel's Day of Atonement is understood to be a future time when their sins will be forgiven as a nation. We today in the Dispensation of Grace had our sins forgiven (that is to say that we have already received the atonement) the day (the moment) we each personally trusted Jesus Christ as Savior (Rom. 5:11). Israel is a covenant nation and thus God deals with them as a nation. They look forward to that day as Peter says at Pentecost: "And now, brethren, I wot that through ignorance ye did *it*, as *did* also your rulers. But those things, which God before had shewed by the mouth of all his prophets, that Christ should suffer, he hath so fulfilled. Repent ye therefore, and be converted, *that your sins may be blotted out, when the times of refreshing shall come from the presence of the Lord;* [emphasis added] And he shall send Jesus Christ, which before was preached unto you: Whom the heaven must receive until the times of restitution of all things, which God hath spoken by the mouth of all his holy prophets since the world began. For Moses truly said unto the fathers, A prophet shall the Lord your God raise up unto you of your brethren, like unto me; him shall ye hear in all things whatsoever he shall say unto you. And it shall come to pass, *that* every soul, which will not hear that prophet, shall be destroyed from among the people." (Acts 3:17-23)

Peter's words in Acts 3:17 ("I wot that through ignorance ye did it.") take us back to Luke 23:34 "Then said Jesus, Father, forgive them; for they know not what they do. And they parted his raiment, and cast lots." (cf. Luke 19:12-14; 20:17-21; Matt. 21:37-38)

In Acts 15:11 "...we [Israel] shall [in the future] be saved even as they [i.e. even as they are now]" we see Peter learning from Paul how it is that Israel's sins will be forgiven. It is there at that Acts Chapter 15 conference that Peter learned what was really accomplished on the cross. We see Peter conveying the same thought in 2Peter 3:14-16.

> "14 Wherefore, beloved, seeing that ye look for such things, be diligent that ye may be found of him in peace, without spot, and blameless. 15 And account *that* the longsuffering of our Lord *is* salvation; even as our beloved brother Paul also according to the wisdom given unto him hath written unto you; 16 As also in all *his* epistles, speaking in them of these things; in which are some things hard to be understood, which they that are unlearned and unstable wrest, as *they do* also the other scriptures, unto their own destruction. 17 Ye therefore, beloved, seeing ye know *these things* before, beware lest ye also, being led away with the error of the wicked, fall from your own stedfastness. 18 But grow in grace, and *in* the knowledge of our Lord and Saviour Jesus Christ. To him *be* glory both now and for ever. Amen." **(2 Peter 3:14-18)**

Peter's words in Acts 3:23 ("every soul, which will not hear that prophet, shall be destroyed from among the people...") take us back to John the Baptist's words in Matthew 3:10 "...every tree which bringeth not forth good fruit is hewn down and cast into the fire..." and 3:12 "...he will burn up the chaff with unquenchable fire."

Israel's sins were paid for by Christ on Calvary but the payment is not applied until He returns to the nation. The redemption of Israel under the New Covenant will be similar to the pattern set in the redemption of Israel out of Egypt into the Promised Land under the Old Covenant. Israel was born as a nation when God redeemed them out of Egypt (Ex. 12:38ff). God made the Old Covenant with the nation in the wilderness (Ex. 19:3-8). God established a priesthood in Exodus 28. The priests then made intercession for the nation. In the parallel application we can see Moses as a type of Christ.

Table 3 Christ and Moses Compared

Moses	Christ
Goes up on a mountain to receive the Law	Goes to a far country to receive a kingdom (Luke 19:12)
Delays his return to the nation	Delays His return to the nation
Israel becomes impatient	Israel gets impatient
Moses finds Israel in idolatry	Christ finds Israel in idolatry (Matt. 12:45, Luke 11:25-26)
Moses makes intercession for the nation (Deut. 9:14-26)	Christ intercedes for the nation as her High Priest in heaven.

There is another important parallel between Israel coming out of Egypt and Israel going into the kingdom. God did promise Israel the kingdom and Israel will go into the kingdom ("...the gifts and calling of God are without repentance" as stated in Romans 11:29). However, it will not be the entire nation that goes into the kingdom just as it was not the entire nation that went into the land in the Exodus. Numbers 14:19-24 speaks of what appears to be a breaking of a promise (Num. 14:34) on God's behalf.

> [19] Pardon, I beseech thee, the iniquity of this people according unto the greatness of thy mercy, and as thou hast forgiven this people, from Egypt even until now. [20] And the LORD said, I have pardoned according to thy word: [21] But *as* truly *as* I live, all the earth shall be filled with the glory of the LORD. [22] Because all those men which have seen my glory, and my miracles, which I did in Egypt and in the wilderness, and have tempted me now these ten times, and have not hearkened to my voice; [23] *Surely they shall not see the land which I sware unto their fathers, neither shall any of them that provoked me see it:* [emphasis added] [24] But my servant Caleb, because he had another spirit with him, and hath followed me fully, him will I bring into the land whereinto he went; and his seed shall possess it." (Num 14:19-24)

> "[34] After the number of the days in which ye searched the land, *even* forty days, each day for a year, shall ye bear your iniquities, *even* forty years, and ye shall know my breach of promise. [35] I the LORD have said, I will surely do it unto all this evil congregation, that are gathered together against me: in this wilderness they shall be consumed, and there they shall die." (Num 14:34-35)

We see a similar apparent "breach of promise" in the book of Acts. Some of that generation died without getting into the kingdom because of their unbelief but their children (a future generation of Israelites) will get into the kingdom. Remember what Hebrews 6:4 said "it is impossible to renew them again to repentance." However, there is no real breach of promise because Israel's High Priest intercedes for the nation and the nation eventually gets into the promised kingdom (Heb. 7:25).

Leviticus 16:15 regarding the Day of Atonement is truly a type of what happened in Acts 3:18 and afterwards. Israel's real Day of Atonement is yet future. The high priestly work of Christ explained in the book of Hebrews explains how it is (how it can be) as though Israel does not exist as God's nation today; that God will preserve them to save them in the future.

Study Guides Questions on the overview of Chapters 8-10

1. Why does Israel need a High Priest?
2. What exactly is the office of the High Priest?
3. How can Christ be a High Priest being that He is not from the tribe of Levi?
4. What does the Lord do for Israel as her High Priest?
5. What is Israel's relationship to Christ as her High Priest?

CHAPTER 8
A BETTER PRIESTHOOD

Hebrews 8:1-2 "Now of the things which we have spoken *this is* the sum: We have such an high priest, who is set on the right hand of the throne of the Majesty in the heavens; ² A minister of the sanctuary, and of the true tabernacle, which the Lord pitched, and not man."

These two verses summarize what is covered in the first seven chapters of the Book of Hebrews dealing with the person of Jesus Christ. From Chapter 8 on to the end of the book, the focus will be on His work. The "we" in this verse is Israel – specifically "we" being the believing remnant of Israel. Verse one is a reference from Psalm 110:1. "¹ The LORD said unto my Lord, Sit thou at my right hand, until I make thine enemies thy footstool." That passage is quoted or referenced in Hebrews five times (1:3, 1:13, 8:1, 10:12-13, and in 12:2).

Verse 2 talks about "the true tabernacle that the Lord pitched:" The book of Hebrews looks back to the tabernacle and not forward to the temple which will come later. The tabernacle was in the wilderness (1Chr. 21:29) while the temple was in the land. The temple typifies the peace that will come to Israel when the Kingdom is set up. However, the tabernacle typifies Israel while she is in the Tribulation period heading to the kingdom. So too, King David and King Solomon are types of Christ. David was a man of war and for that reason was not allowed to build the temple (1Chr. 28:3). Solomon on the other hand then typifies the temple and kingdom glory. In Verse 2 we see that the true tabernacle is in heaven. The Lord Jesus Christ will one day build the temple of the Lord, as we see in Zechariah 6:12-13. "And speak unto him, saying, Thus speaketh the LORD of hosts, saying, Behold the man whose name *is* The BRANCH; and he shall grow up out of his place, and he shall build the temple of the LORD: Even he shall build the temple of the LORD; and he shall bear the glory, and shall sit and rule upon his throne; and he shall be a priest upon his throne: and the counsel of peace shall be between them both."   The temple will be built on earth but the true tabernacle is in heaven as is the true temple. The Lord Jesus Christ will build a temple on earth patterned after that in heaven but not until He begins to reign. Before the kingdom can be established, Christ will have to do His high priestly work of intercession for the nation in the tabernacle in heaven.

John the apostle being given instruction to measure the temple in the Revelation comes to mind here. That incident in the Revelation bears upon the doctrine here in Hebrews Chapter 8.

Revelation 11:1-2
"¹ And there was given me a reed like unto a rod: and the angel stood, saying, Rise, and measure the temple of God, and the altar, and them that worship therein. ² But the court which is without the temple leave out, and measure it not; for it is given unto the Gentiles: and the holy city shall they tread under foot forty *and* two months." (Rev. 11:1 & 2)

In Revelation 11:1-2, John is given a measuring stick and is told to measure the temple, the altar, and the people that worship in it. Taking a measure of something is what one does when he takes possession of it. Here, God is taking possession of the temple, the altar, and the people that worship in it. However, the outer court is not to be measured because it is to be given unto the Gentiles. This indicates that the time frame is after the rapture when God again deals with Israel as being separate from the Gentiles. Today, there is no distinction between the Jew and the Gentile (Eph 2:13-18). Jerusalem is still regarded as the holy city even though it is trodden down of the Gentiles for 42 months yet. The 42 months is three and a half prophetic years (i.e. the second half of the seventieth week of Daniel

Chapter 9). It is note worthy that the temple is rebuilt (Daniel Chapters 8 & 9) during the tribulation period and the temple service is re-established. However, the believing remnant of Israel will recognize that the temple service with its animal sacrifices no longer is the means of justification for them. The temple that is rebuilt during the tribulation period in not the temple referred to in Zechariah 6:12-13 that the Messiah will build. There are five temples that can be indentified in scripture: There is the original temple that Solomon built. There is the temple that the returning remnant built in Ezra and Nehemiah's day. There is the third temple that will be built under the covenant that the unbelieving nation builds with the antichrist in the Tribulation Period. There is the millennial temple that Messiah builds. Finally, there is the temple in heaven (Revelation 11:19; 15:5). The temples that are built on earth are all shadows of the one in heaven.

> **Hebrews 8:3-5** "[3]For every high priest is ordained to offer gifts and sacrifices: wherefore *it is* of necessity that this man have somewhat also to offer. [4]For if he were on earth, he should not be a priest, seeing that there are priests that offer gifts according to the law: [5]Who serve unto the example and shadow of heavenly things, as Moses was admonished of God when he was about to make the tabernacle: for, See, saith he, *that* thou make all things according to the pattern shewed to thee in the mount."

Verse 4 makes an important point regarding Jesus: "...If he were on earth, he should not be a priest..." If Christ were on earth and the Mosaic Covenant were in effect, He could not be a priest. There had to be a change of the Law for Christ to be a priest (Heb. 7:12). The Lord Jesus Christ was called to be a priest by the Father (Heb. 5:4-5). As we see in Numbers 16, it was a serious matter for someone who was not called to the office to intrude into the priest's office (Num. 16:28-36). In 1 Samuel 13:8ff we see that Saul lost the kingdom for intruding into the priest's office. In 2Chronicles 26:16ff we see that Uzziah was struck with leprosy for intruding into the priest's office.

Verse 5 tells us that the Old Covenant was a shadow of heavenly things. The Old Covenant with its tabernacle and temple was a shadow of the New Covenant. So too the earthly things of the Old Covenant were but a type of the heavenly things and the things concerning the New Covenant that is to come. Jesus Christ is the minister of the real things and not the shadowy example.

The Institution of the New Covenant

> **Hebrews 8:6-13** "But now hath he obtained a more excellent ministry, by how much also he is the mediator of a better covenant, which was established upon better promises. [7]For if that first *covenant* had been faultless, then should no place have been sought for the second. [8]For finding fault with them, he saith, Behold, the days come, saith the Lord, when I will make a new covenant with the house of Israel and with the house of Judah: [9]Not according to the covenant that I made with their fathers in the day when I took them by the hand to lead them out of the land of Egypt; because they continued not in my covenant, and I regarded them not, saith the Lord. [10]For this *is* the covenant that I will make with the house of Israel after those days, saith the Lord; I will put my laws into their mind, and write them in their hearts: and I will be to them a God, and they shall be to me a people: [11]And they shall not teach every man his neighbour, and every man his brother, saying, Know the Lord: for all shall know me, from the least to the greatest. [12]For I will be merciful to their unrighteousness, and their sins and their iniquities will I remember no more. [13]In that he saith, A new *covenant*, he hath made the first old. Now that which decayeth and waxeth old *is* ready to vanish away."

Verse 6 begins to talk about the superiority of Christ's ministry: "But now hath he obtained a more excellent ministry..." Christ has:

- A more excellent ministry (Heb. 8:6)
- A better priesthood
- Serves in a better tabernacle (Heb. 8:1-5)
- Administers a better Covenant (Heb. 8:6-13)
- Provides a better service (Heb. 9:1-12)
- Brought a better sacrifice (Heb. 9:13-18).

Verse 7 draws out the point that the first covenant needed to be replaced: "For if that first covenant had been faultless..." speaks of the fact that the Old Covenant could not save Israel from her sins neither could it get Israel into the Kingdom. However, the fault was not with the Old Covenant of the Law. Rather, the fault was with the people. Note: "for finding fault with *them...*" (Emphasis added) The problem is the weakness of human flesh to keep the Law (Rom 8:3).

"I will make a new covenant with the house of Israel and with the house of Judah"
This takes us to Ezekiel 37:15-25 where we see that the two separate nations (Israel and Judah) will become one again. They had been separate nations since 1Kings 11 when Jeroboam led the ten northern tribes of Israel in revolt against Rehoboam the son of Solomon. The Lord speaks of this reuniting of the two nations in John 10:15-16 saying: "As the Father knoweth me, even so know I the Father: and I lay down my life for the sheep. [16] And other sheep I have, which are not of this fold: them also I must bring, and they shall hear my voice; and there shall be one fold, *and* one shepherd." Note the progression of the advance of the kingdom as laid out in Acts 1:8: First it (the gospel) was to go to Jerusalem, then Judea (the two southern tribes), then Samaria (the ten northern tribes), and then the gospel of the kingdom would go to all the world. In Acts 8:14-17 we see this being worked out as the Samarian believers did not receive the Holy Ghost when they believed and were baptized as the believers in Judea had been. What we see happening in Acts Chapter 8 is that God required that Samaria (the ten northern tribes) must recognize Jerusalem as the seat of government in the Kingdom in order for them to receive the Holy Spirit and enter the Kingdom.

Verses 9 through 12 are a direct reference to Jeremiah 31:31 with regard to the promised New Covenant. This New Covenant was ratified on Calvary but will not take effect until the Lord returns to Israel. Under the New Covenant God will do for them what they could not do because of the weakness of the flesh:

Note the eight works that the New Covenant has in them:
1. "I will put my laws into their mind,
2. and write them in their hearts:
3. and I will be to them a God,
4. and they shall be to me a people:
5. And they shall not teach every man his neighbor, and every man his brother, saying, Know the Lord: for all shall know me, from the least to the greatest.
6. For I will be merciful to their unrighteousness,
7. and their sins and their iniquities will I remember no more." (Jeremiah 31:31)

Verse 10 looks to the future: "For this *is* the covenant that I will make..." The New Covenant takes effect when the Lord returns to earth to close the tribulation period. The New Covenant was future from the time of the writing of this epistle of Hebrews and from where we are in time today. This defines the "when" of Acts 3:19 and Romans 11:26.

Acts 3:19 "Repent ye therefore, and be converted, that your sins may be blotted out, ***when*** the times of refreshing shall come from the presence of the Lord..."

Romans 11:26-27 "And so all Israel shall be saved: as it is written, There shall come out of Sion the Deliverer, and shall turn away ungodliness from Jacob: For this *is* my covenant unto them, **when** I shall take away their sins."

However, things are different for us in the dispensation of grace.

Today we have the complete forgiveness of sins according to the riches of God's grace (Eph. 1:7) the very moment that we each individually make the decision to trust Jesus Christ as Savior. This forgiveness is not according to a covenant that God made with anybody "...but according to his own purpose and grace, which was given us in Christ Jesus before the world began... (2Tim. 1:9). Today we do need teachers (1Tim. 5:17) while Israel will not when the New Covenant takes effect. Also, today we do not have a supernatural supply of knowledge by which we can always have a positive response to prayer as Israel will under the New Covenant (Matt. 21:22). Today, we know not what we should pray for as we ought (Rom. 8:26). That will not be the case with Israel under the New Covenant.

1 John 2:20-27 (KJV)

20 But ye have an unction from the Holy One, and ye know all things. ...25 And this is the promise that he hath promised us, *even* eternal life. ... and ye need not that any man teach you: but as the same anointing teacheth you of all things, and is truth, and is no lie, and even as it hath taught you, ye shall abide in him.

Study Guides Questions on Chapter 8

1. The first seven chapters focus on the person of Jesus Christ. What does the rest of the book of Hebrews focus on?

2. What is the difference between what the Tabernacle typified compared to the Temple?

3. What had to change regarding the Law for Christ to be a priest?

4. List five ways in which Christ's ministry is better than the Old Testament types.

5. Why, according to Verse 7 did the Old Covenant have to be replaced?

6. How does Verse 8 relate to the progression of the advance of the Gospel in Acts 1:8?

7. List 8 things that will happen to Israel under the New Covenant according to Jeremiah 31:31.

8. The New Covenant was ratified by Calvary but when will it take effect?

9. Are we today technically under the New Covenant?

CHAPTER 9
A BETTER COVENANT

We will see in Chapter 9 that the New Covenant could not take effect for Israel at least until Calvary (Heb. 9:16). An Outline of Chapter 9:

9:1-10 – The Ordinances of the Old Covenant were just types of the new.
9:11 -15 – A Better Tabernacle
9:16-22 – A Better Priesthood
9:23- 24 – A Better Sacrifice
9:25-10:18 – One Sacrifice of the New replaces the many of the Old.

Hebrews 9:1-5 "Then verily the first *covenant* had also ordinances of divine service, and a worldly sanctuary. ² For there was a tabernacle made; the first, wherein *was* the candlestick, and the table, and the shewbread; which is called the sanctuary. ³ And after the second veil, the tabernacle which is called the Holiest of all; ⁴ Which had the golden censer, and the ark of the covenant overlaid round about with gold, wherein *was* the golden pot that had manna, and Aaron's rod that budded, and the tables of the covenant; ⁵ And over it the cherubims of glory shadowing the mercyseat; of which we cannot now speak particularly."

The first covenant (the Mosaic Covenant) had ordinances that were divine in origin in that they were given by God. They were carried out in a worldly sanctuary (a sanctuary on earth). In Exodus 25 we see that God had given the pattern for the sanctuary to Moses and Moses was then instructed to make it exactly according to the pattern (Ex. 25:40).

The Tabernacle was built with two rooms. The first was the holy place or the sanctuary. It contained the altar of incense, the table of showbread, and the candlestick. The second was called the Holiest of Holies. It contained the golden censer and the mercy seat which was overshadowed by the cherubim that covered the Ark of the Covenant.

The illustration below shows the layout of the tabernacle. Of particular importance at this point to this study of Hebrews is the fact that there were two rooms separated by the veil.

The Tabernacle

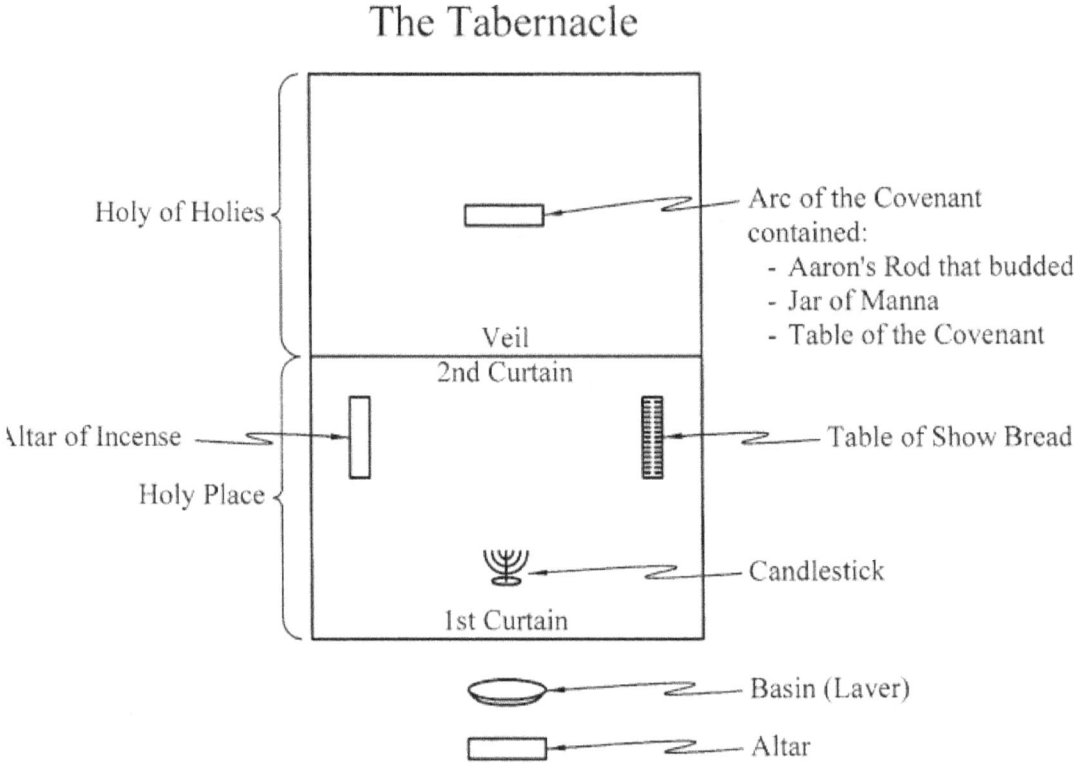

The Tabernacle

Hebrews 9:6-10 "Now when these things were thus ordained, the priests went always into the first tabernacle, accomplishing the service *of God*. [7] But into the second *went* the high priest alone once every year, not without blood, which he offered for himself, and *for* the errors of the people: [8] The Holy Ghost this signifying, that the way into the holiest of all was not yet made manifest, while as the first tabernacle was yet standing: [9] Which *was* a figure for the time then present, in which were offered both gifts and sacrifices, that could not make him that did the service perfect, as pertaining to the conscience; [10] *Which stood* only in meats and drinks, and divers washings, and carnal ordinances, imposed *on them* until the time of reformation."

We note that the verb tenses in this passage describing the chores performed by the priests are all in the past tense. We understand from this that the Old Covenant had (at the time of the writing of the Book of Hebrews) already passed away.

Verse 6 describes the routine chores performed by the priests as being done in the first room of the tabernacle. However, the second room was entered only once per year by the high priest on Israel's annual Feast of Atonement. He entered that second only with a blood sacrifice. First he had a sacrifice for his own sins and then he had another for the sins of the people. Verse 8 describes the significance of the veil separating the first tabernacle (the holy place) from the second (the Holiest of all). The significance is that the sacrifice that really got the job of redemption done was not made yet. This significance is pressed upon us by the fact that the veil was torn from top to bottom the very moment that Jesus died on Calvary (Matt. 27:51-52, Mark 15:38, Luke 23:45). It was then that the real sacrifice was made. However, the truth of that fact was not made known to Israel until the writing of the Book of Hebrews. The passages that follow in Hebrews tell Israel about the fulfillment of the types that were lived out annually by their high priests as they went into the Holiest of all on their annual Feast of Atonement.

Verse 9 speaks of the sacrifices that "...could not make him that did the service perfect, as pertaining to the conscience..." The gifts and sacrifices could not make him that did the service perfect – how much less the people. Note that the issue is the conscience. Conscience is what we know and understand regarding what should be our proper conduct of life. The Old Covenant could make sacrifices for sins but it could not change the man. It could do nothing to the heart of man. The conscience is a function of the heart – the inward man. What the Old Covenant should have taught Israel is that the work of redemption was not finished because it had to be repeated every year. It is noteworthy that one piece of furniture not described in the tabernacle is a chair. There was no place to sit down because the work was never completed under the Old Covenant.

Verse 10 speaks of "...carnal ordinances, imposed *on them* until the time of reformation." The Old Covenant consisted of "meats" (what could and could not be eaten), "drinks" (what could and could not be drunk), "divers washings" (various baptisms or washings – Numbers 19; Leviticus 14; Leviticus 15:6,13,16; Leviticus 16:4,24,26,28; Leviticus 17:16; etc.), and carnal ordinances (things that could be done in and by the flesh). The "time of reformation" is the time when the New Covenant is established to replace the Old. Hebrews will take Israel to that time of reformation when the New Covenant replaces the Old.

> **Hebrews 9:11-14** "But Christ being come an high priest of good things to come, by a greater and more perfect tabernacle, not made with hands, that is to say, not of this building; [12] Neither by the blood of goats and calves, but by his own blood he entered in once into the holy place, having obtained eternal redemption *for us*. [13] For if the blood of bulls and of goats, and the ashes of an heifer sprinkling the unclean, sanctifieth to the purifying of the flesh: [14] How much more shall the blood of Christ, who through the eternal Spirit offered himself without spot to God, purge your conscience from dead works to serve the living God?"

Jesus Christ is the minister of the real tabernacle in Heaven – "...an high priest of good things to come." The earthly one was a type of the real one in heaven. Hebrews 8:5: "See, saith he, *that* thou make all things according to the pattern shewed to thee in the mount." (cf. Ex. 25:40; Num. 8:4; Acts 7:44). The blood of bulls and goats were but types of the real but they did allow God to remit the sins of saints under the Old Covenant on an annual basis based on the Father's faith in the coming shed blood of the Son (Romans 3:25).

Note the contrasts between the type and the real:
- The tabernacle on earth was made with human hands. The tabernacle in which Christ served was not made with human hands.
- The sacrifices of the type were those of goats and calves while the sacrifice that Christ offered was His own blood.
- The type had to be repeated daily (Heb. 7:27) and offered year after year while the service that Christ offered was done once by which He obtained eternal redemption for Israel.

Verse 13 speaks of "...the blood of bulls and of goats, and the ashes of an heifer sprinkling the unclean, sanctifieth to the purifying of the flesh..." Each of these had an Old Covenant significance.
- The **blood of bulls** is what Aaron and his family of high priests brought to cover their own sins
- The **blood of goats** is what was offered annually for the sins of the people on the annual Feast of Atonement
- The **ashes of an heifer** has to do with the ordinance of the red heifer in Numbers 19:18 (cf. Lev. 14:1-8) and was involved in the ceremonial cleansing of water baptism in Israel. God tells Israel regarding the offering of the New Covenant "Then I will sprinkle clean water upon you, and ye shall be clean from

all your filthiness, and from all your idols, will I cleanse you." (Ezek. 36:25). Also see Leviticus 14:6-7 on the Old Testament mode of water baptism. Note that "baptism" is a transliterated Greek word from the New Testament text. The Old Testament uses the word "washings." The "...ashes of an heifer sprinkling the unclean" in Verse 13 is the purification rite of Numbers Chapter 19. This would be the water baptizing work of John the Baptist that he practiced as the Father sent him to Israel to prepare the nation for her Messiah. The "baptism of repentance for the remission of sins" (Mark 1:4) that John performed was a purifying rite ordained by God to get Israel ready for her Messiah.

Verse 14 presents the trinity at work in redemption (note that the blood of Christ is offered through the eternal Spirit to God). The blood of Christ not only purchased redemption for us living in the Dispensation of Grace (Acts 20:28) but it also purchased Israel's as well. The blood that flowed through Jesus' veins was a special kind of blood. Not only was it human, it was also divine. Let's follow the logic on the doctrine of the blood:

- The life is in the blood (Gen. 9:4; Lev. 17:10, 14; Deut. 12:23; John 6:53-54).
- The life that God has is eternal life.
- Therefore, the life that God's blood gives is eternal life.
- The shedding of blood was the surrender of a life.
- Christ surrendered the only perfect life that was ever lived to accomplish redemption for us.
- Christ in resurrection life told His disciples "A spirit hath not flesh and bones as ye see me have." (Luke 24:39). There was no mention of blood. The blood that Christ shed went to the third heaven. Romans 3:25 ought to come into view for us here: Jesus is the one that God the Father "...hath set forth to be a propitiation through faith in his blood, to declare his righteousness for the remission of sins that are past [i.e. of past dispensations – See Genesis 3:15] through faith in his blood." This is the Father's faith in the coming shed blood of the Son which enabled the Father to remit the sins of the believers based on the Old Testament animal sacrifices.

Hebrews 9:15-22 "And for this cause he is the mediator of the new testament, that by means of death, for the redemption of the transgressions *that were* under the first testament, they which are called might receive the promise of eternal inheritance. [16] For where a testament *is*, there must also of necessity be the death of the testator. [17] For a testament *is* of force after men are dead: otherwise it is of no strength at all while the testator liveth. [18] Whereupon neither the first *testament* was dedicated without blood. [19] For when Moses had spoken every precept to all the people according to the law, he took the blood of calves and of goats, with water, and scarlet wool, and hyssop, and sprinkled both the book, and all the people, [20] Saying, This *is* the blood of the testament which God hath enjoined unto you. [21] Moreover he sprinkled with blood both the tabernacle, and all the vessels of the ministry. [22] And almost all things are by the law purged with blood; and without shedding of blood is no remission."

Verse 15 says "He is the mediator of the new testament..." There is a difference between a testament and a covenant. All testaments are covenants but not all covenants are testaments. The difference between the two is found in Verse 17. A testament is a covenant that takes effect only after the death of the testator. The Old Testament was dedicated by the blood of animals. Verses 19-21 describe the blood that dedicated the Old Testament tabernacle. The death that ratified the Old Testament in the earthly tabernacle was that of animals. Remember that the earthly was just a pattern of the heavenly. Hebrews 9:15 describes the propitiation for the remission of sins that are past as does Romans 3:25.

The "New Testament" in Verse 15 pertains to Israel. Jeremiah 31:31-40 prophesies of that New Covenant as does also Ezekiel 36. Let's consider the covenant in detail:

"31 Behold, the days come, saith the LORD, that I will make a new covenant with the house of Israel, and with the house of Judah: 32 Not according to the covenant that I made with their fathers in the day *that* I took them by the hand to bring them out of the land of Egypt; which my covenant they brake, although I was an husband unto them, saith the LORD: 33 But this *shall be* the covenant that I will make with the house of Israel; After those days, saith the LORD, I will put my law in their inward parts, and write it in their hearts; and will be their God, and they shall be my people. 34 And they shall teach no more every man his neighbour, and every man his brother, saying, Know the LORD: for they shall all know me, from the least of them unto the greatest of them, saith the LORD: for I will forgive their iniquity, and I will remember their sin no more." (Jeremiah 31:31-34)

We note:
- This covenant will be made with the house of Israel and the house of Judah
- When it takes effect, God will write His law in their hearts and put it in their inward parts – it will be internalized for them
- He will be their God and they His people
- They will no longer need a teacher for every Israelite will have a supernatural supply of the knowledge of God. Though they will not be teaching each other, they will be teaching the Gentiles.
- God will forgive Israel's iniquity and will no more remember their sins. Israel will know from the Book of Hebrews that it is by the blood of Christ as her High Priest that God can forgive their sins.
- It is the book of Hebrews that moves Israel from their Old Covenant to the New.

Ezekiel 36 speaks of the New Covenant as well. In verses 1-23 of Ezekiel 36 the Lord speaks of the cleansing of the land of Israel. From verse 24 to the end of the chapter, He speaks of the cleansing of the people. It is through the New Covenant that He does that cleansing of the people.

"22 Therefore say unto the house of Israel, Thus saith the Lord GOD; I do not *this* for your sakes, O house of Israel, but for mine holy name's sake, which ye have profaned among the heathen, whither ye went. 23 And I will sanctify my great name, which was profaned among the heathen, which ye have profaned in the midst of them; and the heathen shall know that I *am* the LORD, saith the Lord GOD, when I shall be sanctified in you before their eyes. 24 For I will take you from among the heathen, and gather you out of all countries, and will bring you into your own land. 25 Then will I sprinkle clean water upon you, and ye shall be clean: from all your filthiness, and from all your idols, will I cleanse you. 26 A new heart also will I give you, and a new spirit will I put within you: and I will take away the stony heart out of your flesh, and I will give you an heart of flesh. 27 And I will put my spirit within you, and cause you to walk in my statutes, and ye shall keep my judgments, and do *them*. 28 And ye shall dwell in the land that I gave to your fathers; and ye shall be my people, and I will be your God. 29 I will also save you from all your uncleannesses: and I will call for the corn, and will increase it, and lay no famine upon you. 30 And I will multiply the fruit of the tree, and the increase of the field, that ye shall receive no more reproach of famine among the heathen. 31 Then shall ye remember your own evil ways, and your doings that *were* not good, and shall lothe yourselves in your own sight for your iniquities and for your abominations. 32 Not for your sakes do I *this*, saith the Lord GOD, be it known unto you: be ashamed and confounded for your own ways, O house of Israel. 33 Thus saith the Lord GOD; In the day that I shall have cleansed you from all your iniquities I will also cause *you* to dwell in the cities, and the wastes shall be builded." (Ezekiel 36:22-33)

We note from this passage that the New Covenant involves:

- God re-gathering the nation from the nations wherein He had scattered them (Verse 24).
- He will sprinkle clean water on them (the mode of water baptism -- Verse 25).
- He will cleanse them from their idolatry and their filthiness.
- He will put a new heart and a new spirit within them and in the process He will take the stony (inactive) heart out of them (Verse 26).
- He will put His Spirit within them which will cause them to walk in His statutes and to keep His judgments and to actually do them (Verse 27).
- Israel will then dwell in the land forever.

The New Covenant that Jeremiah and Ezekiel speak of is what the Lord refers to in Matthew 19:27 as "the regeneration". The regeneration is a new beginning. Israel will have a new beginning. This new beginning will be a spiritual rebirth as the Lord told Nicodemus: "Verily, verily, I say unto thee, Except a man be born again, he cannot see the kingdom of God ...Verily, verily, I say unto thee, Except a man be born of water and *of* the Spirit, he cannot enter into the kingdom of God." (John 3:3-5) To be born of the water is to have a physical birth. Israel had a physical birth as a nation when the Lord brought them out of Egypt into the land. It was a water birth at the crossing of the River Jordan. The figure of speech has a personal application as well. Simply having physical life does not give an Israelite eternal life. There has to be a rebirth of the spirit as well. What Israel needed yet to enter the promised kingdom of heaven was a spiritual birth. The New Covenant will give them that spiritual rebirth. God dealt with the nation of Israel on the basis of covenants.

- The Abrahamic Covenant will make Israel a nation.
- The Mosaic Covenant (a conditional covenant) would have qualified the nation to go into the land and into the kingdom. However, they failed under this conditional covenant and therefore God promised them a New Covenant whereby God would do for them what they could not do for themselves. Jeremiah 31:31 (discussed above) speaks of this New Covenant by which He will put His Spirit within them and write His law in their hearts but it does not tell Israel how God can do this (and indeed could not tell them for reasons stated in 1Corinthians 2:8).
- The Palestinian Covenant guarantees Israel the land in spite of her failures under the conditional Mosaic Covenant.
- The Davidic Covenant guarantees Israel the kingdom.
- The New Covenant (actually the New Testament) is what will prepare Israel spiritually to be able to realize the Abrahamic covenant that would give them the land and make them a blessing to the Gentiles. It will also enable them to go into the kingdom that is promised in the Davidic covenant. It will also cleanse them and empower and equip them to be the kingdom of priests.

We Gentiles saved today in the Dispensation of Grace are not under this New Covenant though we are justified by the blood of the New Testament and therefore the New Covenant does affect us. Our relationship to God is on the basis of a special revelation that is called the preaching of Jesus Christ according to the revelation of the Mystery. The Mystery is a body of doctrine that was revealed by our Lord Jesus Christ to the world through the Apostle Paul for this present dispensation of grace (Eph. 3:1-3). The Old Covenant was not made with the Gentiles (Rom. 9:4) but it none the less affected us (note Rom. 3:19: "...Now we know that what things soever the law saith, it saith to them who are under the law: that every mouth may be stopped, and all the world may become guilty before God." So too, the New Covenant will be made with Israel (Jer. 31:31, Heb. 8:8) but it also has an effect that extends to us Gentiles (2Cor. 3:6) in the Mystery program.

> **Hebrews 9: 23-26** "*It was* therefore necessary that the patterns of things in the heavens should be purified with these; but the heavenly things themselves with better sacrifices than these. [24] For Christ is not entered into the holy places made with hands, *which are* the figures of the true; but into heaven itself, now to appear in the presence of God for us: [25] Nor yet that he should offer himself often, as the high priest entereth into the holy place every year with blood of others; [26] For then must he often have suffered since the foundation of the world: but now once in the end of the world hath he appeared to put away sin by the sacrifice of himself."

Verses 19-22 describe the death and the blood that ratified the Old Testament. Verses 23-26, however, describe the blood and the death that ratified the New Testament. The blood of bulls and goats would do for the earthly types of the heavenly things. However, it took Divine Blood to enter into the Holy Place in heaven to accomplish eternal redemption.

While the blood of bulls and goats could dedicate the earthly tabernacle, the heavenly tabernacle had to be dedicated with something better and the New Testament had to be ratified with divine blood. No one could enter that tabernacle except with divine blood. That is the blood by which Christ in His resurrection entered into the heavenly tabernacle. Jesus Christ entered into that heavenly tabernacle once having obtained eternal redemption for us and Israel because He entered with His own divine blood that represented a perfect sacrifice of His own perfect life.

Verse 23 "It was therefore necessary that the [earthly] patterns of things in the heavens **should be purified** with these; but the heavenly things themselves with better sacrifices than these." Israel had many ordinances of purification. The New Testament is about the purifying of the people of Israel.

> **Hebrews 9:27-28** "And as it is appointed unto men once to die, but after this the judgment: [28] So Christ was once offered to bear the sins of many; and unto them that look for him shall he appear the second time without sin unto salvation."

"It is appointed unto man once to die..." Once to die is the normal course of life. This is not intended to be an absolute fact but rather it is a general rule. Some examples illustrate this:

- Lazarus died twice (John 11:43).
- The saints raised in Matthew 27:52 died again.
- Elijah did not die at all (2Kings 2:11) neither did Enoch (Gen. 5:24)

The normal course is that men die and then they face Christ (the judge of all) in judgment. However, there is an event that transpires between the two – resurrection. There are three different mass resurrections in scripture. Saints of this present dispensation will be judged at the Judgment Seat of Christ after the rapture (2Cor. 5:10; 1Cor. 3:13; 2Tim. 2:10-12; etc.). Saints in Israel's program will be judged when Christ returns to earth after the first resurrection of prophesy (Luke 19:13-24, Rev. 20:4; 22:12). The lost of the ages will be raised in the second resurrection to be judged at the great white throne judgment of Revelation 7:9; 22:11.

"So Christ was once offered to bear the sins of many..." (Verse 28) This follows the same logic as Romans 5:15-19 where we see, "And not as *it was* by one that sinned, *so is* the gift: for the judgment *was* by one to condemnation, but the free gift *is* of many offences unto justification."(Rom. 5:16).

Study Guides Questions on Chapter 9

1. Give a simple five point outline of Chapter 9.

2. List the contents of each of the two rooms of the sanctuary.

3. Why are the verb tenses in Verses 6-10 all in the past tense?

4. How often did a priest go into the second room of the Tabernacle?

5. According to Verse 8, what did the rending of the veil in Matthew 27: 1-52 signify?

6. Why the reference to Conscience in Verse 9?

7. Why was there no chair in the furnishings of the old Covenant Tabernacle?

8. What is "the reformation" to which Verse 10 makes reference?

9. What, according to Verse 14, does the blood of Christ do that the Old Testament's sacrifices could not do?

10. List three contrasts between the real Tabernacle in heaven and the type that is on earth.

11. What significance, according to Verse 13, does the ashes of a heifer, and the blood of bulls and goats have to do with Old Covenant?

12. Describe how Verse 14 presents the Trinity at work in redemption.

13. How does the verse of Hebrews 9:15 compare with the verse of Romans 3:25?

14. Describe how the five last covenants (the Abrahamic, the Mosaic, the Palestinian, the Davidic, and the New) relate to Israel.

CHAPTER 10
A BETTR SACRIFICE

Hebrews 10:1-4 "For the law having a shadow of good things to come, *and* not the very image of the things, can never with those sacrifices which they offered year by year continually make the comers thereunto perfect. [2] For then would they not have ceased to be offered? because that the worshippers once purged should have had no more conscience of sins. [3] But in those *sacrifices there is* a remembrance again *made* of sins every year. [4] For *it is* not possible that the blood of bulls and of goats should take away sins."

Verse 1 speaks of "...The law having a shadow of good things to come..." The Law was a shadow of good things to come but it was not the very image of those things to come. The Law presented a general outline of good things to come. We ask, "What are the good things to come of which the Law was a shadow?" Those good things include:

- The forgiveness of sins under the New Covenant that God will make with Israel;
- The clearing of the believer's conscience of sin;
- The removal of the sin nature from the believers in Israel.

All of these things will be realized under the New Covenant. The Law did have a provision for the forgiveness of sin but it did not have a permanent provision. Believers under the Old Covenant still had a conscience of sin even though their sins were remitted.

It is interesting to compare Hebrews 10:1 with Colossians 2:16-17. In Colossians 2:16 the apostle Paul refers to the law saying "Let no man therefore judge you in meat, or in drink, or in respect of an holyday, or of the new moon, or of the Sabbath *days*: Which are a shadow of things to come; but the body *is* of Christ." Paul saw the Law as shadow of things to come but those "things to come" will come after the close of the dispensation of grace. Those things of which the Law was a shadow will come to Israel after the rapture of the church the body of Christ and the Tribulation period that would follow. They are things that will come into fruition with the establishment of the Kingdom of Heaven on earth. The Law was not a shadow of things that we have today in the Dispensation of Grace. We are not under the shadow of the things to come nor are we under the things to come. We are under grace – a parenthesis placed by God between the two.

Peter sheds light on the things that were a shadow of things to come and on the things to come themselves in 1Peter 1: 10-11. "Of which salvation the prophets have enquired and searched diligently, who prophesied of the grace *that should come* unto you: Searching what, or what manner of time the Spirit of Christ which was in them did signify, when it testified beforehand the sufferings of Christ, and the glory that should follow."

Note regarding this passage:

1. The salvation referred to was prophesied. Ours was not (Eph .3:1-4).
2. The prophets themselves searched but could not figure out or discern:
   a. What – i.e. what the prophecy meant.
   b. What manner of time – i.e. the time frame of its fulfillment.

The prophetic passages that speak of the sufferings of Christ include: Isaiah 53, Psalm 22, Jeremiah 30, Zechariah 12 & 13, etc. The sufferings were prophesied but the Old Testament saints could not figure out what they meant. So too, the Old Testament sacrifices were types of the cross but the Old Testament saints did not and could not know it. What God was going to accomplish in and by the cross had to have been kept a secret at least until it was accomplished. First Corinthians 2: 7-8 tells us why " ⁷But we speak the wisdom of God in a mystery, *even* the hidden *wisdom*, which God ordained before the world unto our glory... ⁸which none of the princes of this world knew: for had they known *it*, they would not have crucified the Lord of glory.

Verse 1 says **The Law...can never...make the comers thereunto perfect.** The Law (actually the sacrifices of the Law) can never make those that brought them perfect. The Old Testament sacrifices could remit sin (Rom. 3:25) but could not permanently take away sins. Israel had to maintain an account system for sins. We refer to that as a short account system – a system whereby one keeps track of his short accounts with God. The Old Testament saint had to keep an account of sins and bring the sacrifice every year that would remit those short accounts on an annual basis. If they departed from the Law and failed to do it, they would be in a "lost" state (see Ezek. 18:20-28). If they repented and returned to the Law and brought the blood sacrifice, they would be again reckoned as being "righteous" or "just"(Ezek. 18:21) We today have all of our sins forgiven and have an imputed righteousness (the righteousness of Christ imputed to our account) the instant we trust Christ as Savior (2Cor. 5:21, Rom 3:23-28). At that instant, we have received the atonement (Rom. 5:11) while Israel (nationally) still looks forward to her real Day of Atonement (Rom. 11:26, Acts 3:19, cf. Lev. 16:11, 23:27).

Verse 2 points out the weakness of the Law saying "...the worshippers once purged should have had no more conscience of sins..." There would be no more short account system (i.e. no more conscience of sins) if the Old Testament sacrifices could have taken away sins. There would be no need to keep track of sins and sin would no longer bother you if the account of sin were completely settled. Sin under the Old Testament Law was like an unpaid debt that continually was on the mind. Note in Leviticus 4:1ff that the Old Testament sacrifices made atonement for sin but it was forgiveness on a year by year basis. Leviticus 17:11 "it is the blood [i.e. of bulls and goats] that maketh atonement for the soul."

Hebrews 10:4 - The blood of bulls and goats could not take away sins – they could only cover sins until the real sacrifice was made that got the work of redemption done.

> **Hebrews 10:5-10** "Wherefore when he cometh into the world, he saith, Sacrifice and offering thou wouldest not, but a body hast thou prepared me: ⁶In burnt offerings and *sacrifices* for sin thou hast had no pleasure. ⁷Then said I, Lo, I come (in the volume of the book it is written of me,) to do thy will, O God. ⁸Above when he said, Sacrifice and offering and burnt offerings and *offering* for sin thou wouldest not, neither hadst pleasure *therein*; which are offered by the law; ⁹Then said he, Lo, I come to do thy will, O God. He taketh away the first, that he may establish the second. ¹⁰By the which will we are sanctified through the offering of the body of Jesus Christ once *for all*."

Verse 5 "Sacrifice and offering thou wouldest not..." does not mean that the Father did not want Israel to bring the blood sacrifices. Rather it means that the Father did not send His Son into the world to carry on that Old Testament sacrificial system. This is a direct reference to Psalm 40:6-8. "Sacrifice and offering thou didst not desire; mine ears hast thou opened: burnt offering and sin offering hast thou not required. 7 Then said I, Lo, I come: in the volume of the book *it is* written of me, 8 I delight to do thy will, O my God: yea, thy law *is* within my heart. 9 I have preached righteousness in the great congregation: lo, I have not refrained my lips, O LORD, thou knowest. 10 I have not hid thy righteousness within my heart; I have declared thy faithfulness and thy salvation: I have not concealed thy lovingkindness and thy truth from the great congregation." (Psalm 40:6-10) Note though that Psalm 40:6 says "mine ears hast thou opened…" while Hebrews 10:5 says "…a body thou hast prepared me." The significance of the opened ear is seen in Exodus 21:5-6 where the slave who could go free but chooses to stay with the former master has his ear pierced. The Lord Jesus Christ was given a human body so that He can do the Father's will in sacrificing Himself as the perfect sacrifice.

(In the volume of the book it is written of me...) The entire Bible speaks of and testifies to the Lord's obedience to the Father in the sacrifice of Himself. The will of the Father was that believers be sanctified by the offering of the physical body of Christ as a once for all sacrifice that settled the sin question forever.

"...A body hast thou prepared me." The Son was equipped with a human body so that He could be equipped to bring a perfect sacrifice – the sacrifice of the only perfect human life that has ever been lived. He was a willing sacrifice, a perfect sacrifice, and a complete sacrifice that could both take away the first covenant and that He can establish the second.

> **Hebrews 10:11-14** "And every priest standeth daily ministering and offering oftentimes the same sacrifices, which can never take away sins: 12 But this man, after he had offered one sacrifice for sins for ever, sat down on the right hand of God; 13 From henceforth expecting till his enemies be made his footstool. 14 For by one offering he hath perfected for ever them that are sanctified."

Under the Old Covenant, when an Israelite sinned, that sin was written on an account by God until a sacrifice was brought to remove it. But under the New Covenant, Christ would take away sins once for all by the sacrifice of Himself. Once that sacrifice was made, He sat down at the right hand of God because the work of redemption was done. He will not stand again (speaking figuratively) until it is time for Him to do the work of judgment (See Psalm 110:1; Matt. 22:44; Luke 22:69; Act 2:34 cf. Act 7:56 regarding His current posture and of Him one day standing in judgment).

Verse 14 says "For by one offering he hath perfected for ever them that are sanctified." His one sacrifice of Himself did it all for all time.

> **Hebrews 10:15-18** "*Whereof* the Holy Ghost also is a witness to us: for after that he had said before, 16 This *is* the covenant that I will make with them after those days, saith the Lord, I will put my laws into their hearts, and in their minds will I write them; 17 And their sins and iniquities will I remember no more. 18 Now where remission of these *is, there is* no more offering for sin."

"This is the covenant that I will make with them [Israel] after those days…" and then the quote is a reference from

Jeremiah 31 and Ezekiel 36. The New Covenant will put the law within their hearts and write it in their minds. It will forgive their sins. It will also remove the sin nature from their flesh. All of this will happen for them on their coming real Day of Atonement.

> **Hebrews 10:19-22** "Having therefore, brethren, boldness to enter into the holiest by the blood of Jesus, [20] By a new and living way, which he hath consecrated for us, through the veil, that is to say, his flesh; [21] And *having* an high priest over the house of God; [22] Let us draw near with a true heart in full assurance of faith, having our hearts sprinkled from an evil conscience, and our bodies washed with pure water."

They can have boldness because the blood of Christ did what the Old Covenant sacrifices could not do. It is a new way because it is the New Covenant as opposed to the Old. It is a living way in that it involves perfect righteousness being imputed to them from Christ the source of life. It is once for all because nothing will ever again come between Israel and God. Verse 22 speaks of the faith that clears the conscience from sins – the confidence that the debt of sin is cleared forever.

- A true heart is a heart of faith.
- In "the full assurance of faith" is a statement that we trust in the trustworthiness of Christ's shed blood.
- Having hearts sprinkled from an evil conscience speaks of an inward conviction that sins are indeed forgiven. Peter speaks of this sprinkling in his first epistle:

> "[1] Peter, an apostle of Jesus Christ, to the strangers scattered throughout Pontus, Galatia, Cappadocia, Asia, and Bithynia, [2] Elect according to the foreknowledge of God the Father, through sanctification of the Spirit, unto obedience and sprinkling of the blood of Jesus Christ: Grace unto you, and peace, be multiplied. [3] Blessed *be* the God and Father of our Lord Jesus Christ, which according to his abundant mercy hath begotten us again unto a lively hope by the resurrection of Jesus Christ from the dead, [4] To an inheritance incorruptible, and undefiled, and that fadeth not away, reserved in heaven for you, [5] Who are kept by the power of God through faith unto salvation ready to be revealed in the last time. [6] Wherein ye greatly rejoice, though now for a season, if need be, ye are in heaviness through manifold temptations: [7] That the trial of your faith, being much more precious than of gold that perisheth, though it be tried with fire, might be found unto praise and honour and glory at the appearing of Jesus Christ: [8] Whom having not seen, ye love; in whom, though now ye see *him* not, yet believing, ye rejoice with joy unspeakable and full of glory: [9] Receiving the end of your faith, *even* the salvation of *your* souls. [10] Of which salvation the prophets have enquired and searched diligently, who prophesied of the grace *that should come* unto you: (1Pet 1:1-10)

- Having bodies washed with pure water in Hebrews 10:22 speaks of the outward (external) testimony of repentance (bringing of fruits meet for repentance).

Ezekiel 36:25-38 speaks of that spiritual cleansing under the New Covenant:

> "[25] Then will I sprinkle clean water upon you, and ye shall be clean: from all your filthiness, and from all your idols, will I cleanse you...

> [33] Thus saith the Lord GOD; In the day that I shall have cleansed you from all your iniquities I will also cause *you* to dwell in the cities, and the wastes shall be builded. **...**

36 Then the heathen that are left round about you shall know that I the LORD build the ruined *places, and* plant that that was desolate: I the LORD have spoken *it*, and I will do *it*."

Hebrews 10:23-27 "Let us hold fast the profession of *our* faith without wavering; (for he *is* faithful that promised;) 24 And let us consider one another to provoke unto love and to good works: 25 Not forsaking the assembling of ourselves together, as the manner of some *is*; but exhorting *one another*: and so much the more, as ye see the day approaching. 26 For if we sin willfully after that we have received the knowledge of the truth, there remaineth no more sacrifice for sins, 27 But a certain fearful looking for of judgment and fiery indignation, which shall devour the adversaries."

The Fourth Warning (Hebrews 10:26-31) -- Don't go back to the Old Testament sacrifices but go on to Christ and His sacrifice.

"Let us hold fast..." This is the fourrth warning in the Book of Hebrews. The believing remnant of Israel during the gospel era, and also the believing remnant during the coming tribulation period will have their profession of faith. What they will need to do though to get into the kingdom will be to hold fast to that profession of faith without wavering. Israel was on a performance based acceptance system whereby their faith had to perform. James says much about this departing from the faith. What James calls "the trying of your faith (Jas 1:1-5) is a reference to departing from Christ to turn to the antichrist. What James calls "the perfect Law of Liberty in James 1:25 is the New Covenant. The double minded man in James 1:8 is one who tries to sit on the fence between the two – between going back to the Old Covenant or going on to the New.. The singleness of the eye in Luke 11:34 and Matthew 6:22-24 is faithfulness to endure. Revelation 2:9-10 states their case clearly: "Be thou faithful unto death, and I will give thee a crown of life."

There will be a strong temptation to forsake assembling of themselves together but it will be important that they do so in order to encourage each other to stay the course. To sin willfully after coming to the knowledge of the truth is to go back to the Old Covenant after being instructed on the New. To go back to the Old Covenant sacrifices is to go back to that which has no redeeming value anymore – "there remaineth no more sacrifice for sins..." in that Old Covenant for Israel once this New Covenant is offered to them. See the book "A Study in the Book of the Revelation" by the same author on how the antichrist re-establishes the Old Covenant sacrificial system.

The day that is approaching in Verse 25 is the day of Christ's return (Mal. 4:1; 2 Thess. 1:7-8). Israel must endure in faith through the seventieth week of Daniel Chapter 9 to get to that day in order to get into the kingdom and thus into eternal life.

Verse 27 speaks of judgment and fiery indignation that shall devour the adversary. This is the Gehenna fire that Deuteronomy 32:22 and Matthew 25:25 and 42 speak about. When the Lord spoke of destroying both the body and soul in hell in Matthew 10:28, he was referring to this Gehenna fire. That is fire that the Lord kindles in the Valley of Hinnom (also called Tophet in Isaiah 30:33; Jer. 7:1; et. al.) when He returns to earth to set up His kingdom.

Hebrews 10:28-31 "He that despised Moses' law died without mercy under two or three witnesses: 29 Of how much sorer punishment, suppose ye, shall he be thought worthy, who hath trodden under foot the Son of God, and hath counted the blood of the covenant, wherewith he was sanctified, an unholy thing, and hath done despite unto the Spirit of grace? ³⁰ For we know him that hath said, Vengeance *belongeth* unto me, I will recompense, saith the Lord. And again, The Lord shall judge his people. ³¹ *It is* a fearful thing to fall into the hands of the living God."

The "he" referred to in Verse 29 is an Israelite who departs from his profession of faith and does not endure unto the end (Matt. 10:22). Note that it is said "...he **was** sanctified." It must be remembered that Israel is a covenant nation. God dealt with Israel on the basis of covenants. The whole nation is sanctified but not every Israelite has the faith to endure and therefore not every one of the nation does get into the kingdom and thus into eternal life. The nation was sanctified but individual members could still be lost. For us today, God deals with us individually. We are individually sanctified when we trust Christ as Savior (1Cor. 6:11). We can understand this by going back to the time when Israel was brought out of Egypt. The whole nation was sanctified in Egypt. However, they came out of Egypt as a mixed multitude of believers and unbelievers. It was then at Kadesh that the unbelievers were made apparent (Num. 13:26-14:3).

There will be a future generation of Israelites who will face the same decision that the believers at Pentecost faced. The Old Covenant sacrifices will be re-started during the tribulation period. They will be faced with a decision either to go back to the Old Covenant or go on to the New Covenant just as the believers could in the early Acts period did. Then it will be more tolerable for Sodom and Gomorrah in that day than for the Israelite city that rejects Christ (Matt. 11:23). Matthew 1:21 says God will save His people from their sins, but today, He is saving people who are not His people. In the Tribulation Period there will be people who say they are apostles and are not (Rev. 2:2) and those that say they are Jews and are not (Rev. 2:9).

Verses 30-31 describe the punishment that verse 29 talks about. This is again a reference back to the Gehenna fire of Deuteronomy 32:22. The man in verse 29 "...hath done despite unto the Spirit of grace..." The Spirit of grace is the pouring out of the Holy Spirit that was done in Acts Chapters 1 thru 7. Zechariah 12:10 prophesies about that outpouring. "And I will pour upon the house of David, and upon the inhabitants of Jerusalem, the spirit of grace and of supplications: and they shall look upon me whom they have pierced, and they shall mourn for him, as one mourneth for *his* only *son*, and shall be in bitterness for him, as one that is in bitterness for *his* firstborn." Israel as a nation did do despite unto the spirit of grace when they rejected the testimony of the Holy Spirit through the believers at Pentecost in early Acts. In doing so, the nation counted the blood of Christ an unholy thing. They committed the sin of drawing back to perdition (Heb. 10:30) instead of going "on to perfection" (Heb. 10:6).

> **Hebrews 10:32-36** "But call to remembrance the former days, in which, after ye were illuminated, ye endured a great fight of afflictions; ³³ Partly, whilst ye were made a gazingstock both by reproaches and afflictions; and partly, whilst ye became companions of them that were so used. ³⁴ For ye had compassion of me in my bonds, and took joyfully the spoiling of your goods, knowing in yourselves that ye have in heaven a better and an enduring substance. ³⁵ Cast not away therefore your confidence, which hath great recompence of reward. ³⁶ For ye have need of patience, that, after ye have done the will of God, ye might receive the promise."

The Jewish believers (the Circumcision believers at Jerusalem and believers of the dispersion to whom James, Peter, Jude and John wrote) could relate to the author of the book of Hebrews in suffering persecution. We note that the writer was associated with Timothy in a prison setting in Italy (Heb. 13:23-24). Possible candidates for the authorship of Hebrews could include Mark and Luke and perhaps Apollos (2Tim. 4:11; Col. 4:10; Philemon 24). See Appendix 3 for this writer's conviction as to who wrote the epistle of Hebrews.

"...In heaven ye have a better and an enduring substance." For the Circumcision believers, their inheritance will be on earth but their faithfulness by which they will have it is recorded in heaven. When Christ returns to the earth to set up His Kingdom, He will bring His reward with Him (Rev. 22:12 cf. Luke 12:1; 19:15; Matt. 6:20; etc.).The order of events is:

1. Christ returns to heaven.
2. Christ receives the kingdom.
3. Christ returns to the earth with the kingdom.
4. Christ brings rewards to the kingdom saints.
   - The reward is authority in the kingdom (Luke 19:17).
   - The reward is reserved in heaven (1 Peter 1:4) to be brought to earth when the Lord returns (Rev. 22:12)..
   - In John 14:2 the Lord speaks of His Father's house. That house is, the temple. The temple had rooms where those involved in service there lived. The twelve will have a part in the authority in the kingdom and will live in the Father's house.

They have need of patience to endure in order to get into the kingdom. If they draw back to perdition, the Lord will have no pleasure in them. They will receive the promise only after they have done the will of the Father.

Hebrews 10:37-39 "For yet a little while, and he that shall come will come, and will not tarry. [38] Now the just shall live by faith: but if *any man* draw back, my soul shall have no pleasure in him. [39] But we are not of them who draw back unto perdition; but of them that believe to the saving of the soul."

Study Guides Questions on Chapter 10

1. What are "the good things to come" of which Verse 1 speaks?
2. Was the Law a shadow of the things that we have in the dispensation of grace or was it a shadow of the New Covenant?
3. How does conscience (Verse 2) relate to the short account system that Israel maintained under the Law?
4. Could the blood of bulls and goats actually take away sin? How then could God remit their sins for them bringing the sacrifices?
5. Why, according to verse 10, did the Father prepare a human body for Jesus His Son?
6. Why could Christ sit down after His ascension back to heaven while the Old Testament priests could not sit down?
7. What would be a heart that is sprinkled from an evil conscience in Verse 22?
8. What are the bodies washed with pure water in Verse 22?
9. What is Verse 26 talking about saying there is no more sacrifice for sin?
10. What is the fiery indignation of Verse 27?
11. Who is Verse 29 talking about?
12. Why does Verse 34 tell them of having "a better and more enduring substance" in heaven if the Kingdom of Heaven is to be set up on earth?

CHAPTER 11
THE GREAT CLOUD OF WITNESSES

Hebrews Chapter 11 is often called the faith chapter of the Bible because it presents such a litany of people of faith. Actually it is addressing the need for faith for the Hebrew people who will be facing the trials of the coming tribulation period to enable them to get through it and to go into the kingdom.

> **Hebrews 11:1-3** "Now faith is the substance of things hoped for, the evidence of things not seen. ² For by it the elders obtained a good report. ³ Through faith we understand that the worlds were framed by the word of God, so that things which are seen were not made of things which do appear."

Verse 1 defines faith as the substance of things hoped for [i.e. the promises of God], the evidence [i.e. the proof] of things not seen. This is more of a description of what faith does for the believer – it gives the believer the evidence that what God reveals about the things not yet seen is true. Hebrews 11:13 illustrates this concept pointing out that "These all died in faith, not having received the promises, but having seen them afar off, and were persuaded of *them*, and embraced *them*, and confessed that they were strangers and pilgrims on the earth."

The Lord gives another definition of faith in John Chapter 3. "He that cometh from above is above all: he that is of the earth is earthly, and speaketh of the earth: he that cometh from heaven is above all. And what he hath seen and heard, that he testifieth; and no man receiveth his testimony. He that hath received his testimony hath set to his seal that God is true. For he whom God hath sent speaketh the words of God: for God giveth not the Spirit by measure *unto him*." (John 3:31-34 KJV) Faith is just that very thing – i.e. setting one's seal to the fact that God is true. People talk often about how strong one's faith is. However, the real strength is not in how strongly one trusts but in how trustworthy the thing is in which one trusts.

For a period of about 450 years Israel had not had a revelation from God. That silence was broken when John the Baptizer comes on the scene in Israel. John's ministry was to give Israel a wake up call that God was fixing to speak to them through His Son. Thus the writer of Hebrews tells Israel "God, who at sundry times and in divers manners spake in time past unto the fathers by the prophets, ² Hath in these last days spoken unto us by *his* Son, whom he hath appointed heir of all things, by whom also he made the worlds;" (Hebrews 1:1-2). When the Son speaks, it is the last word. The Book of Hebrews is a call to trust in the finished work of the Son. When the Son speaks, it is God Himself speaking. "For he whom God hath sent speaketh the words of God: for God giveth not the Spirit by measure *unto him*. The Father loveth the Son, and hath given all things into his hand. He that believeth on the Son hath everlasting life: and he that believeth not the Son shall not see life; but the wrath of God abideth on him." (John 3:34-36) John says "If we receive the witness of men, the witness of God is greater: for this is the witness of God which he hath testified of his Son." (1John 5:9) John says further "He that believeth on the Son of God hath the witness in himself: he that believeth not God hath made him a liar; because he believeth not the record that God gave of his Son." (1John 5:10)

No one could have faith were it not for the fact that "God hath spoken..." Paul says, "So then faith cometh by hearing and hearing by the Word of God." (Rom. 10:17). We believers today have faith that is a response to the Word of God. Let's consider Romans 10:17 (which is actually speaking to the Hebrew people). The "hearing" in this passage is figurative. One could equally read it as "hear it." However, it is not just the hearing of the words but the mental grasping of the content of what is read or heard that counts. Today we receive the Spirit by "the hearing of faith..." (Gal. 3:2-5). Let's consider the sequence involved in coming to faith:
1. God speaks to us through His Word.
2. We understand what He said: "The gospel of our salvation..."
3. We (those that are believers) respond by believing but when we believe, we are sealed to eternal life that instant. (Eph. 1:13). However, the faith that the Hebrew people (the audience of the Book of Hebrews) will have to have to get through the tribulation period will be a faith that endures to the end (Matt. 10:22 cf. Heb. 10:36-37). Note that Hebrews 10:37 quotes Habakkuk 2:3-4 (a tribulation passage). Paul quotes only Habakkuk 2:4 "the just shall live by faith..." in Romans 1:17 and Galatians 3:11. The writer of Hebrews quotes both verses 2 and 3 of Habakkuk Chapter 2 because the Book of Hebrews is set in the context of the tribulation and the faith is that which will be required of them to get through it into the kingdom.

Remember that for some four hundred and fifty years Israel had not had a revelation from God. Now, with the writing of Hebrews, Israel had the Word of the Son ("GOD ... Hath in these last days spoken unto us by his Son..." Heb. 1:1-2). When Christ spoke, God Himself was speaking. Jesus Christ fills three offices for Israel: that of a prophet, a priest, and a king. When on earth, He spoke to Israel as the prophet. He will speak to Israel in the tribulation period from heaven as her High Priest. He will then return to Israel as her King. While on earth, He spoke of "the principles of the doctrine of Christ..." However, in the tribulation period, Israel will have to "...go on to perfection..." by listening to "...Him that speaketh from heaven..." (Heb. 12:25) as her high priest.

There is an important distinction between head and heart knowledge of the Word of God. Galatians 3:2-5 speaks of "the hearing of faith..." The hearing of faith is a heart that is receptive to the Word of God. It is the heart belief that produces real and genuine conviction. It is that kind of conviction that Israel will need to get through the tribulation (in standing against the terror of the antichrist) and into the kingdom. God's Word gave Israel a sure hope in the covenant with Abraham, the covenant with David, and the promise of the coming New Covenant. God's faithfulness is all that they had to trust in. They could see the promise only through the eye of faith. It is that faith that will make them approved.

Verse 3 of Hebrews 11 is a tremendous verse for us to meditate upon: "Through faith we understand that the worlds were framed by the word of God, so that things which are seen were not made of things which do appear." Faith is the spiritual perception that a believer has that an invisible, all powerful, all knowing, God created everything that is visible. That spiritual perception leads us to understand that the ultimate reality is not the physical things around us. It gives us the vision to see the invisible and to know that which can only be known by faith. Peter makes some powerful statements on that kind of faith in his epistles.

1Peter 1:7-9 "⁷That the trial of your faith, being much more precious than of gold that perisheth, though it be tried with fire, might be found unto praise and honour and glory at the appearing of Jesus Christ: ⁸Whom having not seen, ye love; in whom, though now ye see *him* not, yet believing, ye rejoice with joy unspeakable and full of glory: ⁹ Receiving the end of your faith, *even* the salvation of *your* souls."

1Peter 1:19-21 "¹⁹We have also a more sure word of prophecy; whereunto ye do well that ye take heed, as unto a light that shineth in a dark place, until the day dawn, and the day star arise in your hearts: ²⁰Knowing this first, that no prophecy of the scripture is of any private interpretation. ²¹For the prophecy came not in old time by the will of man: but holy men of God spake *as they were* moved by the Holy Ghost." What Peter is saying in this is that the written word of God is more authoritative than the words that were spoken audibly from God at the transfiguration in Matthew 17:1-8.

Faith takes God at His word in spite of the opposition to faith that exists in the world around us. The tribulation saints will experience much of such opposition. Hebrews Chapter 11 goes on from here to list the obstacles to faith that they will face and point them to Old Testament examples of others who had successfully dealt with them. Satan is always on point to oppose God and cast obstacles to faith to prevent people from being faithful. Today, his goal is to get believers to not stand in the identity that we (members of the Body of Christ) have in Christ by faith. From Verse 4 on the writer presents a litany of saints who faced situations similar to those that the tribulation saints will face. As we consider each we will see the similarities of the situations.

Hebrews 11:4 "By faith Abel offered unto God a more excellent sacrifice than Cain, by which he obtained witness that he was righteous, God testifying of his gifts: and by it he being dead yet speaketh."

Abel offered a more excellent sacrifice by faith. We understand from this that God had told both Cain and Abel what to bring and how to bring it (for faith cometh by hearing and hearing by the Word of God – Romans 11:17). Abel's sacrifice was a blood offering. The first blood sacrifice was the killing of innocent animals to cover Adam and Eve's sin in Genesis 3. When God accepted offerings, He did it by fire (1Chr. 21:26; Lev. 9:23; 10:1).

Cain brought a sacrifice that certainly was prettier and more appealing to the eye than Abel's. Moreover, Cain worked harder to bring his offering. Cain's offering represents the human good that is presented by religion today instead of the blood, but God looks for the blood sacrifice. The tribulation saints will have to be faithful to stand for the blood sacrifice of Christ in spite of the human good that will be presented by the religion of the antichrist.

Hebrews 11:5-6 "By faith Enoch was translated that he should not see death; and was not found, because God had translated him: for before his translation he had this testimony, that he pleased God. ⁶But without faith *it is* impossible to please *him*: for he that cometh to God must believe that he is, and *that* he is a rewarder of them that diligently seek him."

Enoch was translated that he should not see death. In Genesis 5:22-24 we see that Enoch walked with God after he begat Methuselah three hundred years..." Some kind of a life changing experience happened to him three hundred years before his death. A study of the passages in Genesis in how he named his son tells us what that was – Methuselah (the name) is a compound word which means essentially "he shall go - it shall come." He was warned of judgment that was coming upon the world. Jude Verses 14 thru 18 also tell us of the judgment that he was told would come: "¹⁴And Enoch also, the seventh from Adam, prophesied of these, saying, Behold, the Lord cometh with ten thousands of his saints, ¹⁵To execute judgment upon all, and to convince all that are ungodly among them of all their ungodly deeds which they have ungodly committed, and of all their hard *speeches* which ungodly sinners have spoken against him. [16]These are murmurers, complainers, walking after their own lusts; and their mouth speaketh great swelling *words*, having men's persons in admiration because of advantage. [17]But, beloved, remember ye the words which were spoken before of the apostles of our Lord Jesus Christ; [18] How that they told you there should be mockers in the last time, who should walk after their own ungodly lusts." (Jude 1:14-18) The tribulation saints will also endure mocking when they tell the world of the judgment that will come. Instead of enjoying the highly developed culture of his day (Gen. 4:20-23), he (Enoch) believed God and acted on his faith. The result was that "he pleased God" (cf. Gen. 5:6).

Hebrews 11:6 "But without faith *it is* impossible to please *him*: for he that cometh to God must believe that he is, and *that* he is a rewarder of them that diligently seek him." Faith is taking God at His Word in spite of the oppositions to faith that one faces. Hebrews Chapter 11 is a list of obstacles to faith. Hebrews 12 is a list of people who obtained a good report in spite of the obstacles that they faced.

The question is often asked "what about those that do not know?" Romans 1:19 – 21 addresses this question. "Because that which may be known of God is manifest in them; for God hath shewed it unto them. ... Because that when they knew God they glorified him not as God ... And changed the glory of God into an image..." The lost are the way they are because they forgot God. Psalm 9:17 says on the matter "The wicked shall be turned into hell, and all the nations that forget God." But God is readily found of anyone who will diligently seek Him. "Then shall ye call upon me, and ye shall go and pray unto me, and I will hearken unto you. And ye shall seek me, and find *me*, when ye shall search for me with all your heart." (Jer. 29:12-13) God's Word will not return to Him void. (Isa. 55:5)

> **Hebrews 11:7** "By faith Noah, being warned of God of things not seen as yet, moved with fear, prepared an ark to the saving of his house; by the which he condemned the world, and became heir of the righteousness which is by faith."

Noah was warned of rain – which was something he had not seen before (Gen. 2:6). He acted on his faith and built the ark to the saving of his house. His act of faith also condemned the world and made him an heir of the righteousness of faith. The tribulation saints will need a similar faith.

The Lord tells His disciples that the days of His return will be like the days of Noah (Matt. 24:38-39). Peter draws the same parallel in 1Peter 3:18-22. "[18]For Christ also hath once suffered for sins, the just for the unjust, that he might bring us to God, being put to death in the flesh, but quickened by the Spirit: [19]By which also he went and preached unto the spirits in prison; [20]Which sometime were disobedient, when once the longsuffering of God waited in the days of Noah, while the ark was a preparing, wherein few, that is, eight souls were saved by water. [21]The like figure whereunto *even* baptism doth also now save us (not the putting away of the filth of the flesh, but the answer of a good conscience toward God,) by the resurrection of Jesus Christ: [22]Who is gone into heaven, and is on the right hand of God; angels and authorities and powers being made subject unto him." The long suffering of God waited in the days of Noah while the ark was in preparation for 120 years (Gen. 6:3). The spirits in prison in Verse 19 are the sons of God (angels) in Genesis 6:1 who inter-married with human women. Jude 6 also speaks of these spirits as "...the angels that kept not their first estate but left their habitation..."

> A side note on the comparison of the ark of Noah's day (1Peter 3:21) with water baptism: According to John 10:1-5 (cf. Luke 7:30) water baptism is the door into the kingdom. What the ark was to Noah, water baptism was to the believers in early Acts and will be again to the tribulation saints in the tribulation.

2Peter 2:4 says of the angels that sinned in Noah's day: "God spared not the angles that sinned, but cast them down to hell... [Tartarus]." Just as there was demonic activity trying to foil God's plan for man in Genesis 6, there will again be demonic activity trying to foil the establishment of the kingdom. The same activity was happening during the Lord's earthly ministry to Israel (Matt. 8:16; 8:31; 9:33; 10:8; Mark 1:34, 39; 6:13; 7:26; 16:9, 17). Note how the devils did not want to leave the land of Israel (Matt. 8:31; Mark 5:10). They were apparently under orders from Satan, their leader, to occupy the land of Israel. A study of the language used in Daniel 2:43 & 44 will indicate that the ten kings that will reign with the antichrist are apparently somehow connected with demonic activity. Note in Daniel 2:43 "43 And whereas thou sawest iron mixed with miry clay, they shall mingle themselves with the seed of men: but they shall not cleave one to another, even as iron is not mixed with clay. The "they" that mingle themselves with the seed of men are a reference to the ten toes of the image. They are not the seed of men but they mingle themselves with the seed of men. The ten kings represented by the ten toes are apparently demonic. Just as Noah's faith gave him victory over the demonic activity of his day, so too the tribulation saints will need faith to contend victoriously with the demonic activity in the Tribulation Period.

> **Hebrews 11:8-10** "By faith Abraham, when he was called to go out into a place which he should after receive for an inheritance, obeyed; and he went out, not knowing whither he went. ⁹By faith he sojourned in the land of promise, as *in* a strange country, dwelling in tabernacles with Isaac and Jacob, the heirs with him of the same promise: ¹⁰For he looked for a city which hath foundations, whose builder and maker *is* God."

Abraham responded to God's call to him to leave the land of his birth to go to a land that he never saw or heard of before that time. He dwelt in tents (as did Isaac and Jacob) in that land of promise knowing by faith that it would one day be theirs. Abraham was "...An Assyrian ready to perish..." (Deut. 26:5) and "...served other gods..." (Josh. 24:2). When he was called of God, he was called alone (Isa. 51:2). Here in Hebrews 11:10 we see that he "looked for a city that had foundations whose builder and maker is God." This would be the New Jerusalem which will not appear until Revelation 21:20. Abraham understood that God was going to give him something that was not there yet. The Hebrew people will have to have faith to believe in a kingdom that was not there yet. Remember Hebrews 10:32 & 36 "After ye have done the will of God ye might receive the promises." Lot, though he was a just man, "...lifted up his eyes toward Sodom." (Gen. 13:10). Abraham however, walked in the land but did not build a city. Walking in the land was an action of one who claimed ownership of it (Gen. 13:17). In Job 1:7 and 2:2 we see Satan doing that in the earth – essentially claiming ownership of it.

> **Hebrews 11:11-12** "Through faith also Sara herself received strength to conceive seed, and was delivered of a child when she was past age, because she judged him faithful who had promised. ¹²Therefore sprang there even of one, and him as good as dead, *so many* as the stars of the sky in multitude, and as the sand which is by the sea shore innumerable."

Sarah believed the promise of God (note Gen. 17:15 & 18:11) in spite of the fact that what they believed in was contrary to the laws of nature. God said it and Abraham and Sarah believed it. They took God at His Word and thus became the example of faith that justifies us today (Rom. 4:19-24).

> **Hebrews 11:13-16** "These all died in faith, not having received the promises, but having seen them afar off, and were persuaded of *them*, and embraced *them*, and confessed that they were strangers and pilgrims on the earth. ¹⁴For they that say such things declare plainly that they seek a country. ¹⁵And truly, if they had been

mindful of that *country* from whence they came out, they might have had opportunity to have returned. [16] But now they desire a better *country*, that is, an heavenly: wherefore God is not ashamed to be called their God: for he hath prepared for them a city."

Faith is what Israel will need in the tribulation period to stand against the terror of the antichrist between the time that they believe and the time that they possess the promise. Hebrews 11:13 is an illustration of Hebrews 11:1 "... faith is the substance of things hoped for, the evidence of things not seen." These all died in faith not having received the promise but nonetheless trusted in the faithfulness of God who made the promise. All of the people from verses 13 through 29 died without having seen the fulfillment of their hope yet through the eye of faith they did see the future fulfillment of it.

Verse 16 takes us back to Joshua leading the children of Israel into the Promised Land. That event is a type of the children of Israel one day going through the tribulation period and into the kingdom. The faith that they will then have is expressed in 1John 4:2-4. Confessing that Jesus Christ has come in the flesh has meaning only in the context of the Tribulation Period when there will be false christs and the antichrist claiming to be Israel's messiah. The true believers of Israel will be telling the nation that the true Christ is the one presented in Matthew, Mark, Luke and John and at Pentecost in the Book of Acts. That same Jesus Christ is being presented to them in the Book of Hebrews as Israel's Redeemer and High Priest.

Jesus Christ is the real Joshua that the Joshua of which Joshua 3:10ff was only a type. Note the important parallel and the significance of the sequence in the transition:

1. The sequence starts with the death of Moses who is a type of and representative of the Old Covenant that God made with Israel. This is a type of the Law being done away to allow the bringing in of the New.
2. Joshua leads the people into the land – a type of Christ leading the people of Israel into the kingdom and the New Covenant.
3. In Joshua 3:11 God is "Lord of all the earth..." and as such he leads Israel into the land. This is the beginning of God reclaiming the earth to Himself.
4. In 2Chroniclaes God is "The LORD God of heaven..." and the kingdoms of the earth are given into the hands of the Gentiles as Israel is taken out of the land and taken into captivity. This is the fifth course of judgment of which Leviticus 26 speaks.
5. In Daniel 2:44 it is as the "God of heaven" that He sets up a kingdom in the earth. God will do for Israel what Israel failed to do for herself.
6. In Matthew's gospel the kingdom is referred to as the Kingdom of Heaven (Matt. 3:2; etc.). In Mark and Luke, it is the Kingdom of God (Mark. 1:14, 15; 4:11; Luke 4:43; 6:20; 7:28; etc.).
7. Here in Hebrews 11:16, it is a heavenly kingdom in the sense that the God of Heaven sets it up and then God's will is gong to be done in the earth as it is in heaven (Matt. 6:9-10).
8. In 1Peter 1:4, this kingdom is "reserved in heaven for you [believers of Israel] but it will be brought by Christ to the earth (Rev. 22:12).

Hebrews 11:17-19 "By faith Abraham, when he was tried, offered up Isaac: and he that had received the promises offered up his only begotten *son*, [18] Of whom it was said, That in Isaac shall thy seed be called: [19] Accounting that God *was* able to raise *him* up, even from the dead; from whence also he received him in a figure."

Here the faith of Abraham is presented to the Hebrew believers. It is interesting that just as James goes to the circumcised Abraham (James 2:22) while Paul goes to the uncircumcised Abram, the writer of Hebrews goes to the incident in Genesis 22:1ff also. Abraham knew that the promised seed of Genesis 3:15 would be his seed. He knew also that the seed would be called in Isaac (Gen. 21:12). He also had come to believe in the resurrection (Gen. 17:8): He and his seed would have the land for an everlasting possession but he would die before he gets it (Gen 15:12-15). Because he believed in the resurrection, Abraham passed the test when he was tried. That will be the same faith that the tribulation saints will need (Rev 2:10).

Hebrews 11:20 "By faith Isaac blessed Jacob and Esau concerning things to come."

Jacob received the blessing of the Abrahamic Covenant from Isaac. The blessing that Jacob received was from God. The blessing that Isaac gave Esau was Isaac's own blessing. By tradition, the elder should get the blessing. However, in this case the younger received it. Isaac realized that he had given the blessing to the younger and the younger received the blessing contrary to tradition. Isaac's faith was expressed in Genesis 27:33 in his words "and he shall be blessed". Isaac trembled knowing and understanding that God had overruled him.

Hebrews 11:21 "By faith Jacob, when he was a dying, blessed both the sons of Joseph; and worshipped, *leaning* upon the top of his staff."

This blessing of the sons of Joseph is in Genesis 48:1ff. The specific blessing is in Genesis 48:15-17.

Hebrews 11:22 "By faith Joseph, when he died, made mention of the departing of the children of Israel; and gave commandment concerning his bones."

In Genesis 50:23 we see that Joseph saw Ephraim's children to the third generation. In Genesis 50:24 Joseph said: "God will surely visit you, and ye shall carry up my bones from hence." Joseph was here expressing faith in the Abrahamic Covenant that there would be deliverance and that there would also be a resurrection based on God's word to Abraham in Genesis 15:1ff.

Hebrews 11:23 "By faith Moses, when he was born, was hid three months of his parents, because they saw *he was* a proper child; and they were not afraid of the king's commandment."

Moses' parents understood from Genesis 15:16 that in the fourth generation, God would deliver Israel out of Egypt. Note the generations in Exodus 6:16-20:

- Jacob begat Levi both of whom went into Egypt –the 1st generation.
- Levi begat Kohath – the 2nd generation.
- Kohath begat Amram – the 3rd generation.
- Amram begat Moses – the 4th generation.

It was Moses' parent's faith that there would be a deliverer in that generation that brought them to the point of faith that they did hide Moses.

Hebrews 11:24-28 "By faith Moses, when he was come to years, refused to be called the son of Pharaoh's daughter; 25 Choosing rather to suffer affliction with the people of God, than to enjoy the pleasures of sin for a season; ²⁶ Esteeming the reproach of Christ greater riches than the treasures in Egypt: for he had respect unto the recompence of the reward. ²⁷ By faith he forsook Egypt, not fearing the wrath of the king: for he endured, as seeing him who is invisible. ²⁸ Through faith he kept the passover, and the sprinkling of blood, lest he that destroyed the firstborn should touch them."

We learn from the account that Stephen gives in Acts 7:21-28 that Moses understood he would be a deliverer of Israel from Egypt (Ex. 2:11-15). He thought that Israel would have understanding of this, too. However he was mistaken on what Israel actually understood yet at that time.

Verse 26 speaks of the reproaches of Christ. No one before the cross understood about the sufferings of Christ (Luke 18:31-34). However, Moses suffered the same reproaches from Israel that Christ would later suffer at Israel's hand. See 1Peter 1:7-10 on what the prophets did and did not know. See also Psalm 69:7-9 on how "...the reproaches of them that reproached thee fell on me..." -- speaking of Christ.

Verse 27 "...for he endured, as seeing him who is invisible." – faith is the means whereby one can see the invisible by believing the word of God.

> **Hebrews 11:29-31** "By faith they passed through the Red sea as by dry *land*: which the Egyptians assaying to do were drowned. ³⁰ By faith the walls of Jericho fell down, after they were compassed about seven days. ³¹ By faith the harlot Rahab perished not with them that believed not, when she had received the spies with peace."

All of these accounts have to do with Israel leaving Egypt and entering the Promised Land. God opened the Red sea so that Israel could pass through and they did pass through by faith. God brought the walls of Jericho down but only after Israel marched around it according to God's word seven days by faith. Rahab had faith to believe that Israel was God's people and acted by faith to save the Israelite spies with the result being the salvation of herself and her family.

> **Hebrews 11:32-38** "³²And what shall I more say? for the time would fail me to tell of Gedeon, and *of* Barak, and *of* Samson, and *of* Jephthae; *of* David also, and Samuel, and *of* the prophets: ³³ Who through faith subdued kingdoms, wrought righteousness, obtained promises, stopped the mouths of lions, ³⁴ Quenched the violence of fire, escaped the edge of the sword, out of weakness were made strong, waxed valiant in fight, turned to flight the armies of the aliens. ³⁵ Women received their dead raised to life again: and others were tortured, not accepting deliverance; that they might obtain a better resurrection: ³⁶ And others had trial of *cruel* mockings and scourgings, yea, moreover of bonds and imprisonment: ³⁷ They were stoned, they were sawn asunder, were tempted, were slain with the sword: they wandered about in sheepskins and goatskins; being destitute, afflicted, tormented; ³⁸ (Of whom the world was not worthy:) they wandered in deserts, and *in* mountains, and *in* dens and caves of the earth."

Each of the heroes of faith in these verses could warrant paragraphs to cite their exploits. What is noteworthy though is that some of them by faith were delivered and others had faith and yet were not delivered.

> **Hebrews 11:39-40** "And these all, having obtained a good report through faith, received not the promise: ⁴⁰ God having provided some better thing for us, that they without us should not be made perfect."

The term "be made perfect" has reference to receiving the object of their faith – i.e. the Messianic kingdom.

Study Guides Questions on Chapter 11

1. Jesus spoke as a prophet while He was on earth, and will speak as a king when he returns to earth but when does He speak as a Priest?
2. What two purposes does faith serve according to Verse 1?
3. What does faith give the believer in Verse 3?
4. In Verse 4, what was the basic difference between Cain's and Abel's sacrifices?
5. According to Verse 6, what two things are required in order to come to God for salvation?
6. Is Chapter 11 about faith or is it more about the obstacles to faith that people overcome?
7. How is Verse 11 an illustration of Verse 1?
8. What is different about people of faith in Verses 4 through 12 from those people of faith in Verses 13 through 27?
9. How does 1John 4:2-4 have real meaning only in the Tribulation Period?
10. How was Joshua's entrance into the land a type of Jesus leading Israel into the kingdom?

CHAPTER 12
PATIENTLY RUNNING THE RACE

Hebrews 12:1 "Wherefore seeing we also are compassed about with so great a cloud of witnesses, let us lay aside every weight, and the sin which doth so easily beset *us*, and let us run with patience the race that is set before us, ² Looking unto Jesus the author and finisher of *our* faith; who for the joy that was set before him endured the cross, despising the shame, and is set down at the right hand of the throne of God."

Jesus Christ did everything that He needed to do for the Hebrews to be able to have redemption and eternal life. What the Hebrew people had to do now was to put their trust in Jesus the author and the finisher of their faith.

The Fifth Warning is in the verses that follow (most specifically in Verses 3 – 29).

Hebrews 12:3-6 "For consider him that endured such contradiction of sinners against himself, lest ye be wearied and faint in your minds. ⁴ Ye have not yet resisted unto blood, striving against sin. ⁵ And ye have forgotten the exhortation which speaketh unto you as unto children, My son, despise not thou the chastening of the Lord, nor faint when thou art rebuked of him: ⁶ For whom the Lord loveth he chasteneth, and scourgeth every son whom he receiveth."

Consider the contrast of the only human being that was not only innocent but who was absolutely intrinsically righteous dying for the sins of the worst of men. The theme of this chapter is the chastening of the Lord. Verses 5 and 6 are references to Proverbs 3:11-12. There are two reasons for the Lord's chastening: He loves them, and they (the Israelites) are His children. The chastening in view here is the Tribulation Period. In Exodus 4:22 God instructs Moses to say unto Pharaoh, "Thus saith the LORD, Israel *is* my son, *even* my firstborn:" Israel is God's son among the nations. The tribulation is the chastening of that nation to bring the Lord's son to the maturity that the nation must have to be the means of being the blessing to the Gentile nations that God intended it to be.

Hebrews 12:7-8 If ye endure chastening, God dealeth with you as with sons; for what son is he whom the father chasteneth not? ⁸ But if ye be without chastisement, whereof all are partakers, then are ye bastards, and not sons."

The Book of Hebrews, as the first book of the Hebrew church epistles, is written to instill in the Hebrews the faith that will get them through the tribulation that will come on earth and which the nation will endure. The Hebrew who endures chastening is the son of the Father. Israel is to know that they are God's sons because He does chasten them. If one is not chastened, he is not a son. Job 5:17 says "Happy is the man whom God correcteth therefore despise not thou the chastening of the Almighty."

We need to consider the difference between chastening and punishment.
Chastening is loving discipline applied to produce proper conduct.
Punishment is the penalty imposed for an infraction of rules.
Retribution is wrath for sins and offenses.

There is a series of chastenings that God was going to bring on Israel under the Old Covenant. We see them in Leviticus 26:14-41. They are actually referred to as successive courses of chastisement that are designed by God to bring the nation to maturity as God's son. These sequential courses of chastisement actually form the layout of

Israel's History from the giving of the Law through to the establishment of the kingdom. The successive courses of judgment are laid out as follows:

1. Leviticus 26: 16-17 covers the chastisement that comes during period of the Judges thru Solomon's reign.
2. Leviticus 26: 18-20 is the chastisement that is covered in 1Kings
3. Leviticus 26:21-22 is covered in 2Kings thru Chapter 11
4. Leviticus 26:23-26 is covered in 2Kings Chapter 11 thru 16
5. Leviticus 26: 27-39 is covered in 2Kings 16 through to the Book of the Revelation and the Tribulation Period. This fifth course of chastisement was interrupted by the present dispensation of grace. The Times of the Gentiles began in this course when Israel was taken captive in Babylon. The Book of Daniel introduces this fifth course.

Leviticus 26:40 – 46 then tells Israel how she can get out form under the chastening. "If they shall confess their iniquity..." In Daniel Chapter 9:20 we see Daniel doing that very thing. He (and the heart attitude he manifests) is an example of what the Tribulation saints will be doing. John the Baptist's work was to bring Israel to the point of repentance (See Matt. 3:3; Mark 1:4; Luke 3:3; Acts 13:34; etc.) Leviticus 26:41-42 says "...If their uncircumcised heart be humbled...Then will I remember my covenant with Jacob, and with Isaac, and also my covenant with Abraham will I remember; and I will remember the land..." Stephen, in bringing his indictment in Acts 7:51was looking for such repentance in Israel. Peter preached a baptism of repentance in Acts 2:38 in hopes of seeing that repentance. Neither Stephen nor Peter saw that repentance that was needed in Israel. However, that repentance will come one day at the close of the tribulation. The prophet Zechariah describes the desired repentance it in Zechariah 12:11-14

"[11] In that day shall there be a great mourning in Jerusalem, as the mourning of Hadadrimmon in the valley of Megiddon. [12] And the land shall mourn, every family apart; the family of the house of David apart, and their wives apart; the family of the house of Nathan apart, and their wives apart; [13] The family of the house of Levi apart, and their wives apart; the family of Shimei apart, and their wives apart; [14] All the families that remain, every family apart, and their wives apart."

Zechariah 12:11-14

In Isaiah 32:1-15 we see a fore view of the New Testament Hebrew Scriptures:

- Verse 1 "Behold, a king shall reign in righteousness..." This is Jesus Christ.
- "...princes shall rule in judgment." These will be the twelve apostles who will sit on twelve thrones judging the twelve tribes of Israel (cf. Matt. 19:28).
- Verse 6 "For the vile person will speak villany, and his heart will work iniquity, to practice hypocrisy, and to utter error against the LORD, to make empty the soul of the hungry, and he will cause the drink of the thirsty to fail." This is describing the career of the antichrist.
- Verses 13 & 14 "Upon the land of my people shall come up thorns *and* briers; yea, upon all the houses of joy *in* the joyous city: Because the palaces shall be forsaken; the multitude of the city shall be left; the forts and towers shall be for dens for ever, a joy of wild asses, a pasture of flocks..." This will be the land lying desolate until Israel is brought back into it when Israel's feasts of Trumpets and Tabernacles are realized.
- Verse 15 "Until the spirit be poured upon us from on high, and the wilderness be a fruitful field, and the fruitful field be counted for a forest." This is the establishment of the New Covenant and the kingdom.

Hebrews 12:9-10 "Furthermore we have had fathers of our flesh which corrected *us*, and we gave *them* reverence: shall we not much rather be in subjection unto the Father of spirits, and live? [10] For they verily for a few days chastened *us* after their own pleasure; but he for *our* profit, that *we* might be partakers of his holiness."

Correction done by human fathers is done so that they can be pleased with the product of their labor in their children. Chastening of the Lord, however, is done so that the children can be partakers of His holiness. The Lord chastens his people so that they can be what God created man to be – the eternal custodians of His creation (Heb. 2:5-7).

Hebrews 12:11-13 "Now no chastening for the present seemeth to be joyous, but grievous: nevertheless afterward it yieldeth the peaceable fruit of righteousness unto them which are exercised thereby. [12] Wherefore lift up the hands which hang down, and the feeble knees; [13] And make straight paths for your feet, lest that which is lame be turned out of the way; but let it rather be healed.

Israel will be healed in the chastening of the Tribulation Period. The writer encourages them to endure that which is coming on them.

Hebrews 12:14 "Follow peace with all *men*, and holiness, without which no man shall see the Lord:"

This exhortation tells us the tribulation saints will be peace loving people. Without peace and holiness no man shall see the Lord. This is an interesting verse. In Revelation 1:7 it says that every eye shall see Him. In Revelation 6:16 unbelievers see Him sitting on a throne. The seeing here in Verse 14 is the seeing of Hebrews 9:28 "So Christ was once offered to bear the sins of many; and unto them that look for him shall he appear the second time without sin unto salvation." This will be the fulfillment of Matthew 5:8: "Blessed are the poor in spirit for they shall see God."

Hebrews 12:15-17 "Looking diligently lest any man fail of the grace of God; lest any root of bitterness springing up trouble *you*, and thereby many be defiled; [16] Lest there *be* any fornicator, or profane person, as Esau, who for one morsel of meat sold his birthright. [17] For ye know how that afterward, when he would have inherited the blessing, he was rejected: for he found no place of repentance, though he sought it carefully with tears."

Esau is presented in scripture as an example of one who loved the present world but had so little regard for the birthright of the Covenant with Abraham that he gave that birthright away for a bowl of soup. Esau was a secular person who had no real interest in the things of God. In the context of Hebrews, to fail the grace of God is to go back to the Old Covenant (Chapter 6). To fail here is to not put one's faith in the New Covenant that God has for the nation. Such a person is a member of the Covenant nation but is not putting his/her faith in the Covenant. God will be offering the New Covenant during the Tribulation Period but Satan will be offering them the Old Covenant and the Old Covenant sacrifices again.

A "Root of bitterness" of which Verse 15 speaks would be as Esau who lost hope of seeing any merit in the covenant that God had made with the nation as the seed of Abraham.

Hebrews 12:18-24 "For ye are not come unto the mount that might be touched, and that burned with fire, nor unto blackness, and darkness, and tempest, [19] And the sound of a trumpet, and the voice of words; which *voice* they that heard intreated that the word should not be spoken to them any more: [20] (For they could not endure that which was commanded, And if so much as a beast touch the mountain, it shall be stoned, or thrust through with a dart: [21] And so terrible was the sight, *that* Moses said, I exceedingly fear and quake:) [22] But ye are come unto mount Sion, and unto the city of the living God, the heavenly Jerusalem, and to an innumerable company of angels, [23] To the general assembly and church of the firstborn, which are written in heaven, and to God the Judge of all, and to the spirits of just men made perfect, [24] And to Jesus the mediator of the new covenant, and to the blood of sprinkling, that speaketh better things than *that of* Abel."

To unpack this passage, we look at eight things that the Hebrew people are come to in the Book of Hebrews.

1. They are come to Mount Zion - 12:18-22.
   - Not the physical Mt. Zion (Verse 18).
   - Definitely not Mt. Sinai (Verses 18-22).
   - They are come to Mount Zion in the Sides of the North (Psalm 48:1&2).
   - Christ will come from Mount Zion (Psalm 50:2&3).
   - The 144,000 will be caught up to the Heavenly Mount Zion (Rev. 14:1).
   - Satan was once there (Ezek. 28:14).
   - There will be a Mid-Tribulation view of Mount Zion (Matt. 16:63; 26:64; Rev. 6:14-17).
   - Christ comes from the North (Psalm 75:4-6).
   - The Jerusalem above is free and is entered on the basis of freedom. Abraham entered that way (Gal. 3:26-28; 4:26).

2. They are come to the City of the Living God (Heb. 11:16; 12:22).

3. They are come to an innumerable company of angels (Heb. 1:14; 12:22).

4. The General Assembly and Church of the Firstborn.
   - "Firstborn" is a title signifying inheritance and resurrection (Col.1:18).
   - Israel is God's firstborn (Ex. 4:22; Jer. 31:9).
   - Christ is the Firstborn among many brethren (Rom. 8:29) and the Firstborn of every creature (Col. 1:15). He is the firstborn from the dead (Col. 1:18).

5. To God the Judge of All (1Peter 1:5; Rev. 14:6).

6. The Spirits of Just Men Made Perfect (Ezek. 18:5-9; 27-30) – made perfect by the New Covenant.

7. To Jesus the Mediator of the New Covenant (Heb. 8:6).

8. To the Blood of Sprinkling (Ex. 24:8).

Unlike the Old Covenant where the people of Israel came to the mount that made them (including Moses himself) exceedingly afraid, the Hebrew people of the Tribulation period will be coming to the heavenly Jerusalem where they can be made perfect (righteous) by the New Covenant.

The Fifth Warning is stated in Hebrews 12:25-39 – Don't refuse Him who now speaks from Heaven

Hebrews 12:25-27 "See that ye refuse not him that speaketh. For if they escaped not who refused him that spake on earth, much more *shall not* we *escape*, if we turn away from him that *speaketh* from heaven: [26] Whose voice then shook the earth: but now he hath promised, saying, Yet once more I shake not the earth only, but also heaven. [27] And this *word*, Yet once more, signifieth the removing of those things that are shaken, as of things that are made, that those things which cannot be shaken may remain."

If they did not escape who refused the one who spoke on earth (Moses), they surely will not escape if they refuse the Lord who speaks now from heaven. God once shook the earth but the time is coming when He will shake both heaven and earth.

Hebrews 12:28-29 "Wherefore we receiving a kingdom which cannot be moved, let us have grace, whereby we may serve God acceptably with reverence and godly fear: [29] For our God *is* a consuming fire."

The "we" of verse 28 is redeemed Israel – the Hebrew people to whom the book of Hebrews is addressed. God is a consuming fire that burns up the slag and purifies the gold. That is what God will do in Israel in the Tribulation Period.

Study Guides Questions on Chapter 12

1. What was it according to Verse 2 that produced faith in the Hebrews?
2. State what the theme of Chapter 12 is based on Verses 3-6.
3. According to Verse 8, what would it mean if one was not chastened of God?
4. How is chastening different from punishment and retribution?
5. Where in scripture do we find the series of chastening that God meted out on the Hebrews?
6. What is the fifth of those successive courses of chastisement?
7. What Verse in Leviticus tells the Hebrews how to get out from under the fifth course?
8. John the Baptist, Stephen, and Peter each called Israel to repentance but did any of them see that repentance? Will that repentance ever come? When?
9. What Old Testament passage describes prophetically Israel's future repentance?
10. What Old Testament passage gives a fore view of the New Testament scripture?
11. What, according to Verse 10, is the difference between the discipline of human fathers and the chastening of the Lord?
12. Is the seeing of Verse 14 the same seeing as Revelation 6:16?
13. What would be the root of bitterness of Verse 15?
14. List eight things that the Hebrew people are come to in the Book of Hebrews.
15. Verses 25 through 29 gives the fifth warning in Hebrews. What is it?

CHAPTER 13
BROTHERLY LOVE

Hebrews 13:1 "Let brotherly love continue."

Love (i.e. the unconditional kind of love) is or ought to be the characteristic of a child of God. It is the fruit of the Spirit in us today (Gal. 5:22). The flesh can not produce it. It has to come from God's work in the believer through His Word. The service that the believer renders to God is said to be a "work and labour of love..." (Heb. 6:10). Jesus taught and commanded His disciples to so love and that love is the hallmark of a true believer (John 13:34). At Pentecost, the believers were filled with the Holy Ghost and manifested that love (Act 2:46-47) in interpersonal relationships among themselves. The apostle John has much to say on the subject of love: In his first epistle, he describes the love that is the outworking of the New Covenant as it impacts the believer. Note his words:

- **1John 2:10-11 (KJV)**
  [10] He that loveth his brother abideth in the light, and there is none occasion of stumbling in him. [11] But he that hateth his brother is in darkness, and walketh in darkness, and knoweth not whither he goeth, because that darkness hath blinded his eyes.
- **1John 3:10-11 (KJV)**
  [10] In this the children of God are manifest, and the children of the devil: whosoever doeth not righteousness is not of God, neither he that loveth not his brother. [11] For this is the message that ye heard from the beginning, that we should love one another.
- **1John 3:14-18 (KJV)**
  [14] We know that we have passed from death unto life, because we love the brethren. He that loveth not *his* brother abideth in death. [15] Whosoever hateth his brother is a murderer: and ye know that no murderer hath eternal life abiding in him. [16] Hereby perceive we the love *of God*, because he laid down his life for us: and we ought to lay down *our* lives for the brethren. [17] But whoso hath this world's good, and seeth his brother have need, and shutteth up his bowels *of compassion* from him, how dwelleth the love of God in him? [18] My little children, let us not love in word, neither in tongue; but in deed and in truth.
- **1John 4:7-8 (KJV)**
  [7] Beloved, let us love one another: for love is of God; and every one that loveth is born of God, and knoweth God. [8] He that loveth not knoweth not God; for God is love.
- **1John 4:20 (KJV)**
  [20] If a man say, I love God, and hateth his brother, he is a liar: for he that loveth not his brother whom he hath seen, how can he love God whom he hath not seen?
- **1John 5:1 (KJV)**
  [1] Whosoever believeth that Jesus is the Christ is born of God: and every one that loveth him that begat loveth him also that is begotten of him.

Hebrews 13:2 "Be not forgetful to entertain strangers: for thereby some have entertained angels unawares."

The Strangers (that being a non-Hebrews) is actually the brother referred to in Verse one. God instructs Israel regarding these strangers in Leviticus 19:34: "*But* the stranger that dwelleth with you shall be unto you as one born among you, and thou shalt love him as thyself; for ye were strangers in the land of Egypt: I *am* the LORD your God." Also note in the Lord's instruction in Deuteronomy 10:18-19 "He doth execute the judgment of the fatherless and widow, and loveth the stranger, in giving him food and raiment. Love ye therefore the stranger: for ye were strangers in the land of Egypt."

Verse 2 suggests that: "Some have entertained angels unawares..." That is an interesting prospect. If you were not aware that a person you had met was an angel, would it not behoove you to reflect on how you had treated him? There have been many such incidences in the Bible where men had entertained angels or where there was an exchange between angels and men. However as we study these incidences, we see that they were always involved with God's program with Israel. The following list is an interesting study on the matter:

- In 2Kings 2:11 – An angelic chariot of fire takes Elijah to heaven.
- In 2Kings 6:17 – Angelic chariots of fire protect Elisha.
- In Isaiah 66:15 - There will be chariots at the return of Christ to earth.
- In Genesis 18:1-10 - Abraham meets the Lord and two angels.
- In Genesis 19:1-3 - Lot entertained angels in Sodom.
- In Genesis 28:10-23 - Jacob sees angels ascending on a ladder from Bethel to heaven.
- In Matthew 13: 41 - Angels will gather the unbelievers out of Israel.
- In Matthew 18:10 – We see that Hebrew children have guardian angels.
- In Matthew 24:7, 31, and 40 - Angels will gather the elect of Israel.
- In Acts 11:13 - An angel had Cornelius send for Peter.
- In Acts 12:1-15 - An angel delivers Peter from prison.

However, today in the Dispensation of Grace, we do not find such angelic intervention. What we find in the Pauline epistles is that angels are learning about the wisdom of God by observing the actions of the believers of this dispensation as they grow to maturity under grace (Eph. 3:10; Col. 1:16). The Law was "ordained by angels..." (Gal. 3:19) and was spoken by angels (Heb. 2:2). However, the Law was weak in that human flesh could not keep it. However, the wisdom of God is manifest in that God's grace can and will produce in the believer of the dispensation of grace the righteousness that the law demanded but could not produce (Rom. 8:3-4). As a result, angels are learning about the wisdom of God through grace put into practice through us (Eph. 3:10). It is the regenerating work of the Holy Spirit (Titus 3:5) and the restraining love of Christ (2Cor. 5:14) that compels us to live out the practical righteousness that the Law demanded but could not produce in us. It is "...the law of the Spirit of life in Christ Jesus" that sets us "Free from the law of sin and death (Rom. 8:2)

> **Hebrews 13:3** "Remember them that are in bonds, as bound with them; *and* them which suffer adversity, as being yourselves also in the body."

This will be important instruction during the tribulation period. There have been many times in Bible history when it was necessary to minister to saints in prison: Some such examples include:

- The story of Joseph in prison (Gen. 40:13-23).
- Ebed-melech who rescued Jeremiah from the prison of Malchiah (Jer. 38:6-13).
- Gentiles who treat imprisoned Israelites well during the tribulation period will enter the kingdom as a reward for their service (Matt. 25:35ff).
- The Philippian jailer treated the apostles well for the message that they carried (Acts 16:29-34).
- So too, Felix treated Paul well for the message that he carried (Acts 24:23).
- Paul was a prisoner for the message that he carried (Eph. 4:1).

- Paul asked for prayer and help because of his bonds (Col. 4:18).
- The Philippians communicated (ministered to his needs) with Paul while he was in prison (Phil. 4:14-15).
- Onesiphorous (and his house) refreshed Paul while he was in prison even though all of Asia had forsaken him (2Tim. 1:16-18).

The words "...As bound with them..." is the expression of empathy. Paul instructs us to rejoice with them that do rejoice and to weep with them that weep (Rom. 12:15). Empathy is an important characteristic in the believer and a mark of spiritual maturity. Paul tells us "whether one member suffer, all the members suffer with it; or one member be honored, all the members rejoice with it." (1Cor. 12:26)

"...As being yourselves also in the body..." is not a reference to being in the Body of Christ as 1Corinthians 12:26 does. These Hebrew people are members of the nation of Israel -- a different elect agency than the church which is Christ's Body. This reference to being "also in the body" is a statement as to how intimate the empathy of a believing Hebrew ought to be for another believing Hebrew who was suffering adversity.

Hebrews 13:4 "Marriage *is* honourable in all, and the bed undefiled: but whoremongers and adulterers God will judge. "

"Marriage is honourable in all..." God ordained marriage as an institution for the propagation of the human race in a secure environment for the rearing of children. God created all the angels as free moral agents but all indication is that There is no procreation among angels in that they neither marry nor are given in marriage (Matt. 22:30). However, when He created man as a free moral agent, He created him male and female so that they could procreate more free moral agents (Gen. 1:27). God's design was that this was to be done in the context of marriage (Gen. 2:21-25).

"The marriage bed undefiled..." God would have husbands and wives (one man with one woman married to each other in a public testimony of the marriage covenant) freely enjoy their sexuality that God created for that purpose. Proverbs 5:15-23 says it well "Drink waters out of thine own cistern, and running waters out of thine own well. ¹⁶ Let thy fountains be dispersed abroad, *and* rivers of waters in the streets. ¹⁷ Let them be only thine own, and not strangers' with thee. ¹⁸ Let thy fountain be blessed: and rejoice with the wife of thy youth. ¹⁹ *Let her be as* the loving hind and pleasant roe; let her breasts satisfy thee at all times; and be thou ravished always with her love. ²⁰ And why wilt thou, my son, be ravished with a strange woman, and embrace the bosom of a stranger? ²¹ For the ways of man *are* before the eyes of the LORD, and he pondereth all his goings. ²² His own iniquities shall take the wicked himself, and he shall be holden with the cords of his sins. ²³ He shall die without instruction; and in the greatness of his folly he shall go astray."

"But whoremongers and adulterers God will judge." God does not take violation of the marriage covenant lightly. For us today in the dispensation of grace, the local church is to judge this sin of adultery by excommunicating the offending parties (1Cor. 5:13). God will judge the unbeliever at the Great White Throne. For Israel under Law, God administers judgment upon sin in this life (Deut. 3:16). For us members of the church which is Christ's Body, judgment for such conduct will be at the Judgment Seat of Christ (2Cor. 5:10) where the result will be suffering loss (1Cor. 3:15) of rewards one could have had for living according to the Word of Grace.

Hebrews 13:5-6 "*Let your* conversation *be* without covetousness; *and be* content with such things as ye have: for he hath said, I will never leave thee, nor forsake thee. ⁶So that we may boldly say, The Lord *is* my helper, and I will not fear what man shall do unto me."

The believer need not fall into the sin of covetousness if he realizes that his God will never leave him or forsake him. The Bible says a lot about covetousness in warning against it. The tenth commandment says, "Thou shalt not covet thy neighbor's house, thou shalt not covet thy neighbor's wife, nor his manservant, nor his maidservant, nor his ox, nor his ass, nor any thing that *is* thy neighbor's." (Ex. 20:17). Covetousness is a serious matter with God:

- Israel before the captivity was totally given to covetousness (Jer. 6:13; Ezek. 33:31).
- Covetousness is one of the sins that come out of the heart of man (Mark 7:22).
- The seed among the thorns are choked by covetousness for the things of this world and result in the Hebrews caught in it being excluded from getting into the kingdom (Luke 8:14).
- Covetousness was one of the characteristics of man as a result of being given up by God (Rom. 1:29).
- Covetousness is one of the six sins for which a professing believer is to be dis-fellowshipped (1Cor. 5:11-13).
- Covetousness is one of the ten characteristics of the old man (who will not inherit the kingdom of God) listed in 1Corinthians 6:10 cf Ephesians 5:1-2).
- An elder in a local church must be free of covetousness (1Tim. 3:1-3)...
- And there are many more verses on the matter.

"I will never leave thee nor forsake thee" is a promise that God made to Jacob in Genesis 28:15. See also Deuteronomy 31:6-8. With God being with them, the Hebrew people need not fear man.

- God pledged to protect the nation (Gen. 28:15).
- Israel was not to fear any man when the nation walked with God (Josh. 1:5).
- Samuel reminds Israel of this (1Sam. 12:22).
- David reminds Solomon of this (1Chr. 28:20).
- David reminds all Israel of this (Psalm 37:25-28).
- The prophets continually remind Israel that God has an eternal purpose for the nation and that He will see to it that that eternal purpose is carried out (Isa. 41:10-17; cf. Isa. 52:4; 14:26-27; 23:9).
- God expanded His eternal purpose with the revelation of the mystery through Paul to include a purpose Body in the heavens m—that purpose being for the church which is Christ's (Eph. 3:11).

Hebrews 13:7-8 "Remember them which have the rule over you, who have spoken unto you the word of God: whose faith follow, considering the end of *their* conversation. [8] Jesus Christ the same yesterday, and to day, and for ever."

The term "them that rule over you..." is used three times in this chapter:

- In Verse 17 they were to obey them that have rulership in the circumcision assembles and submit to them that they may lead with joy.
- In Verse 24 they were to salute them that ruled in the assembly as an expression of respect.
- Here in Verse 7 they were to remember them and follow their faith. These men are motivated by true conviction that Jesus Christ is the eternal unchanging God and act on that conviction (Matt. 24:45 cf. Luke 12:41-48).

We ask, "Were there local circumcision churches when the Book of Hebrews was written?" Yes! We read of seven of them in the first three chapters of the Revelation. These rulers have spoken unto them the Word of God. They were to follow the faith of their leaders by considering the end result of their activity – to represent Jesus Christ as the unchanging God. These Hebrews were people who heard the Word of God spoken with power by men who were filled with the Holy Ghost (Act 4:31). Stephen is an example of such leaders (Act 7:55-60). The Word of God is the testimony of Jesus Christ (Rev. 1:9 cf. Rev. 6:9). In the coming Tribulation period (which the target audience of the Book of Hebrews will face) it will be the Word of God that will be the issue between eternal life and eternal death (Rev. 20:4). The Word of God is quick (i.e. it is alive because the Holy Ghost who gave it is ever present to use it to produce faith), it is powerful (it can get the job done) and sharper than any two edged sword, and it can distinguish between soul and spirit in man (Heb. 4:12-13). This is something that the natural man cannot do (1Cor. 2:16). Today in the dispensation of grace it is the same – it is the Word that does the work of saving souls (Rom. 10:17; 1Thess. 2:13).

Verse 8 "Jesus Christ the same yesterday and today and forever…" is a statement that He is the unchanging God. During His earthly ministry to Israel, He told the unbelieving scribes and Pharisees: "Verily, verily, I say unto you, Before Abraham was, I am." (John 8:58). Psalm 102:25-28 describes the unchanging nature of God "Of old hast thou laid the foundation of the earth: and the heavens *are* the work of thy hands. They shall perish, but thou shalt endure: yea, all of them shall wax old like a garment; as a vesture shalt thou change them, and they shall be changed: But thou *art* the same, and thy years shall have no end. The children of thy servants shall continue, and their seed shall be established before thee." Because Jesus Christ is the unchanging God, Israel can have hope of deliverance during the Tribulation period. The prophets assured Israel that because God does not change, the sons of Jacob will not be consumed (Mal. 3:6). God's word to them is "Grace be unto you and peace from him which is and which was, and which is to come…" (Rev. 1:4).

> **Hebrews 13:9** "Be not carried about with divers and strange doctrines. For *it is* a good thing that the heart be established with grace; not with meats, which have not profited them that have been occupied therein."

Verses 9 through 13 are talking about the New Covenant that God will make with Israel. The writer is telling the Hebrew people to maintain doctrinal purity. In Matthew's Gospel the Lord warned Israel of the great deception that would come in the Tribulation period: "⁴ And Jesus answered and said unto them, Take heed that no man deceive you. ⁵ For many shall come in my name, saying, I am Christ; and shall deceive many." (Matt. 24:4-5). "For there shall arise false Christs, and false prophets, and shall shew great signs and wonders; insomuch that, if *it were* possible, they shall deceive the very elect. Behold, I have told you before." (Matt. 24:24-25)

John tells the Tribulation saints how to test the spirits. "Hereby know ye the Spirit of God: Every spirit that confesseth that Jesus Christ is come in the flesh is of God: And every spirit that confesseth not that Jesus Christ is come in the flesh is not of God: and this is that *spirit* of antichrist, whereof ye have heard that it should come; and even now already is it in the world." (1John 4:2-3) There will be spirits (prophets) who will be pointing to some man who is alive then and who will be claiming to be Jesus Christ. However, the truth will be that Jesus Christ had come in the flesh and had died for their sins, and was buried, and rose again the third day and is then seated at the Father's right hand. The doctrine of Hebrews regarding the high priestly work of Christ will be the doctrine that saves them (Heb. 9:23-28; 10:8-14). He will sit at the Father's right hand until it is time to make His enemies His footstool (Heb. 10:12; Act 2:34; Col. 3:1; Heb. 1:3,13; Act 7:56; Luke 19:12, etc.).

> **Hebrews 13:10** "We have an altar, whereof they have no right to eat which serve the tabernacle."

These Hebrew people are going to be asked by God to go on from the Old Covenant which "…stood only in meats and drinks, and divers washing..." to the New Covenant (Heb. 9:9-12). In doing so, they are "...going on to perfection" (Heb. 6:1) to an altar (Calvary) that they which serve the Old Testament tabernacle (established by the Law in Num. 3:7-8) have no right to eat of. God met with Israel in a tabernacle on earth under the Old Covenant. That tabernacle was constructed according to the pattern in heaven (Ex. 25:9; Num. 8:4). That tabernacle on earth was a shadow of the real tabernacle established in heaven under the New Covenant (Heb. 8:6).

> **Hebrews 13:11-12** "For the bodies of those beasts, whose blood is brought into the sanctuary by the high priest for sin, are burned without the camp. [12] Wherefore Jesus also, that he might sanctify the people with his own blood, suffered without the gate."

Verse 11 is a reference back to Numbers 4:5-12 regarding the sin offering. The man who brought the offering killed the offering (Verse 4 of Numbers 4 -- this makes sense for us as well for Christ is our sin offering and we killed Him because of our sin). The priest then took the blood into the tabernacle (Verses 5-7) to place it on the mercy seat. Hebrews 10:26-31 speaks of the seriousness of counting the blood of Christ an unholy thing. While the blood was taken into the tabernacle, the body of the offering is then taken outside the camp and burned (Verses 10–12). Verses 16–21 of Numbers 4 prescribes the same procedures for open sin of the congregation. The result is that the sin (whether individual or congregational) shall be forgiven (Numbers 4:20). All sin offerings were to be burned – never eaten (Lev. 9:9-11).

Aaron, as the high priest of Israel, had to bring a sin offering for himself (Lev. 9:9-11). All of the priests after the order of Aaron (Lev. 7:11-19) had to do the same (Lev. 5:3; 7:27). However, Jesus Christ did not have to offer a sacrifice for His own sin for He had no sin. However He offered His own blood for the sins of His people (Heb. 9: 8-15; 1Peter 1:2). Leviticus 16:14-27 describes the same basic procedure to be followed on Israel's annual Day of Atonement. In Numbers 19 we see also that the body of the red heifer also was burned outside of the camp.

> **Hebrews 13:13-16** " Let us go forth therefore unto him without the camp, bearing his reproach. [14] For here have we no continuing city, but we seek one to come. [15] By him therefore let us offer the sacrifice of praise to God continually, that is, the fruit of *our* lips giving thanks to his name. [16] But to do good and to communicate forget not: for with such sacrifices God is well pleased."

"Let us go forth therefore onto Him without the camp..." In other words: let us (the believing remnant of Israel) go forth to him without the camp (i.e., outside of the Judaism of Israel and the Old Covenant). Christ suffered and shed the blood of the New Covenant (Luke 23:32-33) outside the camp to indicate that the believer in Israel had to leave the Old Covenant and embrace the New Covenant in order to enter into life (Heb. 12:24). The Old Testament sacrifice no longer had any redeeming value (Heb. 10:26) now that the New Covenant sacrifice has been made (Heb. 10:29).

Hebrews 11:26 makes an interesting statement of Moses. He esteemed the reproach of Christ greater riches than the treasures of Egypt. Christ suffered reproach (1Tim. 4:10) and so will His followers. Moses suffered the same reproach before Christ did. It is the reproach that all suffer for believing that God has a plan of redemption that calls people out of the riches and comforts of the world to suffer reproach for the purpose of a future blessing in God's kingdom. Hebrews 12:2 describes our Lord's foresight that enabled Him to endure the reproach. The Lord tells His followers of the reproaches they will suffer (Matt. 5:11; 10:24-25; 16:24). The true leader who will lead God's people knows how to suffer reproach (1Cor. 4:10-13) as Paul did. Paul learned to take pleasure in reproaches for Christ's sake (2Cor. 12:10).

In Verse 14 we see that the Hebrew people seek a continuing city that is yet to come. They seek a continuing city because when the book was written (and continuing to this day) they had no city on earth. Abraham looked for a city whose builder and maker is God (Heb. 10:10). All who looked for that city (as Abraham, Isaac, and Jacob did) "...died in faith, not having received the promises, but...embraced them and confessed that they were strangers and pilgrims on earth. "...They desire a better country, that is, a heavenly..." (Heb. 11:12-16). The doctrine of Hebrews takes them "...unto Mount Zion, and unto the city of the living God, the heavenly Jerusalem...to the general assembly and church of the first born..."

> **Hebrews 13:17** "Obey them that have the rule over you, and submit yourselves: for they watch for your souls, as they that must give account, that they may do it with joy, and not with grief: for that *is* unprofitable for you."

It is an awesome responsibility to have rulership in an assembly of believers. Those who do will give an account to the Lord one day for their actions. Here the writer enjoins the Hebrew believers to not cause them grief but rather that they might find joy in their work. See the comment on Verse 7 above.

> **Hebrews 13:18-21** "Pray for us: for we trust we have a good conscience, in all things willing to live honestly. [19] But I beseech *you* the rather to do this, that I may be restored to you the sooner. [20] Now the God of peace, that brought again from the dead our Lord Jesus, that great shepherd of the sheep, through the blood of the everlasting covenant, [21] Make you perfect in every good work to do his will, working in you that which is wellpleasing in his sight, through Jesus Christ; to whom *be* glory for ever and ever. Amen."

This closing salutation encourages the believers to do good works that please God. The book of Hebrews carries no authorship indications within the text. However, it is apparent that these Hebrews who received it knew well who it was who wrote the book. It appears from Verses 18 and 19 that the writer is in some type of confinement by the civil authorities. We will discuss more on this in Appendix 3.

> **Hebrews 13:22** "And I beseech you, brethren, suffer the word of exhortation: for I have written a letter unto you in few words."

We trust that the author is speaking of this letter to the Hebrews when he speaks of a letter written in few words. However one can't help but wonder if he is not talking about some other letter for this can hardly be said to be a letter written in few words. This is a book of doctrine regarding the high priestly work of Christ to Israel, a Book of warning (Verses 5:11-6:12; 10:26-37; 12:3-17), as well as a book of exhortation.

> **Hebrews 13:23-25** "Know ye that *our* brother Timothy is set at liberty; with whom, if he come shortly, I will see you. [24] Salute all them that have the rule over you, and all the saints. They of Italy salute you. [25] Grace *be* with you all. Amen."

It appears that the letter was written from Italy in a prison setting in which Timothy had been confined with the author. This gives us some clues as to who wrote the letter. See Appendix 3 for further information.

Study Guides Questions on Chapter 13

1. What is the source of love in Verse 1?
2. Who would be a stranger referred to in Verse 8?
3. When we find angels interacting with men in the Bible, which of God's programs are they involved with?
4. What is the nature of angelic interaction with men today inn the dispensation of grace?
5. What does it mean "as being yourselves in the body?"
6. What does Verse 4 say about violation of the marriage contract?
7. Who would they be that rule over the Hebrew believers in Verses 7 and 8?

APPENDIX

Appendix 1 – The Target Audience of the Book

Appendix 2 – The Doctrinal Position of the Book in the New Testament

Appendix 3 -- History to Prophecy it is all His Story

Appendix 4 – The Authorship of the Book

APPENDIX 1
THE TARGET AUDIENCE FOR HEBREWS

The Book of Hebrews is addressed to Hebrew people who were to go on to perfection (Heb. 6:1-4) from the salvation message that at first began to be spoken by the Lord (Heb. 2:3). The perfection of their salvation message was in the high priestly work of Christ (Heb. 2:17; 3:1; 4:14-15; 5:1,5,10; 6:20; 7:1, 26, 27, 28; 8:1,3; 9:7; 11:25; 10:21; 13:11). Hebrews presents the blood atonement of Christ in the context of the prophetic program with Israel. The doctrine of Hebrews will take Israel through the coming Tribulation period and culminate in the Book of the Revelation to take the nation into the promised Kingdom.

The Book of Hebrews does for these Hebrew people what the Book of Romans does for us in the Dispensation of Grace. We have redemption through His blood (Eph. 1:7; Col. 1:14). We find that doctrine first in Romans 3:21-25. The twelve preached "gospel" (Luke 9:6) but they did not (during the earthly ministry of Christ) even understand that Christ was going to die, let alone what He was going to die for (Luke 18:34). What gospel then were they preaching? They were preaching the "gospel of the kingdom" (Matt. 4:23; 9:35; 24:14). The cross had not happened yet so how could they have known what was going to be accomplished there. What was accomplished by the crucifixion of Christ had to be kept a secret from the princes of this world for had they known it, they would not have crucified the Lord of Glory (1Cor. 2:8). Those that heard Him had to go on to perfection by learning what was accomplished on the cross. The Book of Hebrews does for the Hebrews what the Book of Romans does for us – it presents the blood atonement in the context of the respective programs.

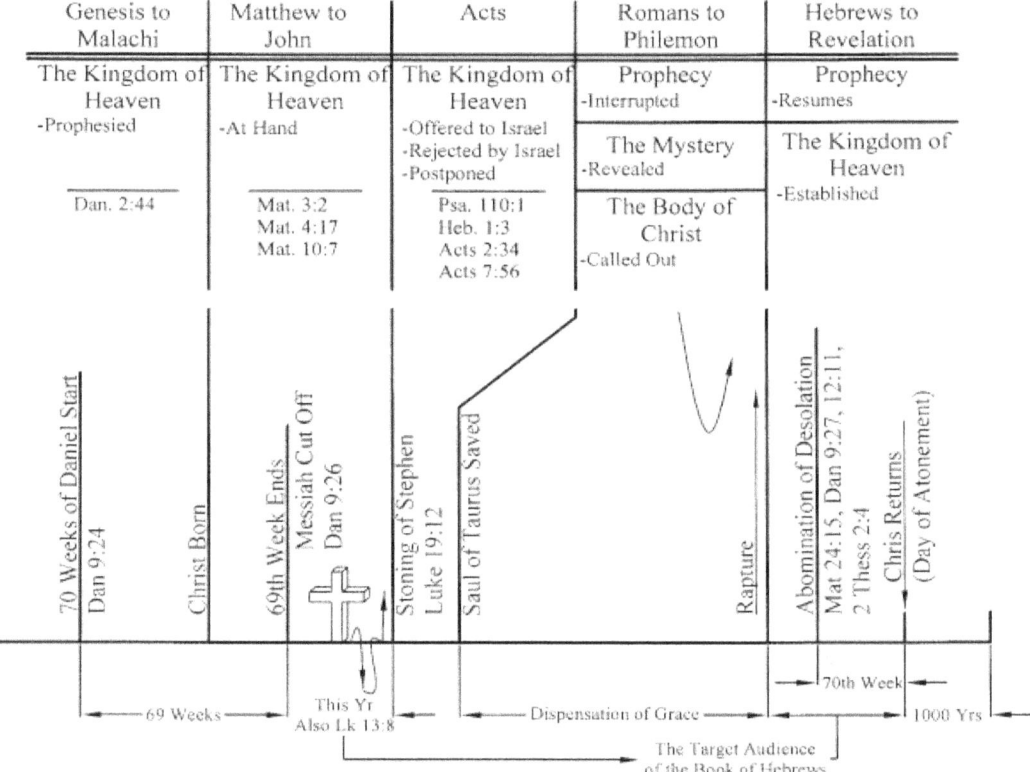

APPENDIX 2 -- THE NEW TESTAMENT SCRIPTURE—RIGHTLY DIVIDED

The New Testament scriptures start with the account of our Lord's earthly ministry in the four Gospels of Matthew, Mark, Luke and John. Following that is the Book of Acts. Then we have what is called the Pauline Epistles (Romans through Philemon). Finally we have the Hebrew church Epistles of Hebrews through the Revelation. That is how we find them laid out in our New Testament. That is actually how the themes of the books unfold in time. The earthly ministry of our Lord Jesus Christ is presented first regarding His ministry to the twelve apostles of Israel. The book of Acts continues with the ministry of the twelve to the nation until mid Act when we find a marked change with the saving of Saul of Tarsus and his call to be the apostle of the Gentiles. The New Testament then has the Pauline Epistles containing a markedly different focus. There the focus in not on Israel but rather it is a broad based outreach to the lost masses of humanity. The elect agency that we find in the Pauline Epistles is no longer the nation of Israel but rather the church which is Christ's Body and the focus is on the dispensation of the grace of God. The apostle Paul calls the message in these epistles "the preaching of Jesus Christ according to the revelation of the mystery." The Book of Romans presents the foundational information to Israel that will equip the nation with the doctrine on how the cross pertains to their program of redemption as God picks up His dealings with them again. Hebrews through the Revelation then takes Israel through the Tribulation Period that follows the dispensation of grace and into the promised Kingdom of Heaven.

Half of the New Testament scriptures are about Israel and God's plan for that nation while the other half is about the Church which is Christ's Body – a Gentile church. The body of doctrine that pertains to Israel is called Prophecy. It is called prophecy because it is what "…God hath spoken by the mouth of all His Holy Prophets since the world began" (Acts 3:21). The other half of the New Testament scriptures (the portion written by Paul, the apostle of the Gentiles) is called the Mystery because it is the body of doctrine that our Lord kept secret until He revealed it to us through Paul for us who live in this present Dispensation of Grace. Paul refers to it as " …The mystery which from the beginning of the world hath been hid in God who created all things by Jesus Christ" (Eph. 3:9). When Paul, the apostle of the Gentiles ,tells us to study to show ourselves approved unto God and be workmen who need not to be ashamed, he is talking about rightly dividing the word of truth – Making the distinction between Prophecy and the Mystery.

The central person in the Bible is our Lord Jesus Christ. He is the creator of all things in heaven and in earth (Col. 1:16). He is also the one who will reconcile everything in heaven and in earth back to Himself (Col. 1:20). There are two programs by which He will do that. Prophecy is the program by which He reconciles the earth to Himself. The Mystery deals with His reign in the heavens. Point by point the two program are different. The table on the facing page points out those differences. When we note the significance of the differences, we begin to understand how important rightly dividing the Word of Turth is to understanding the Bible

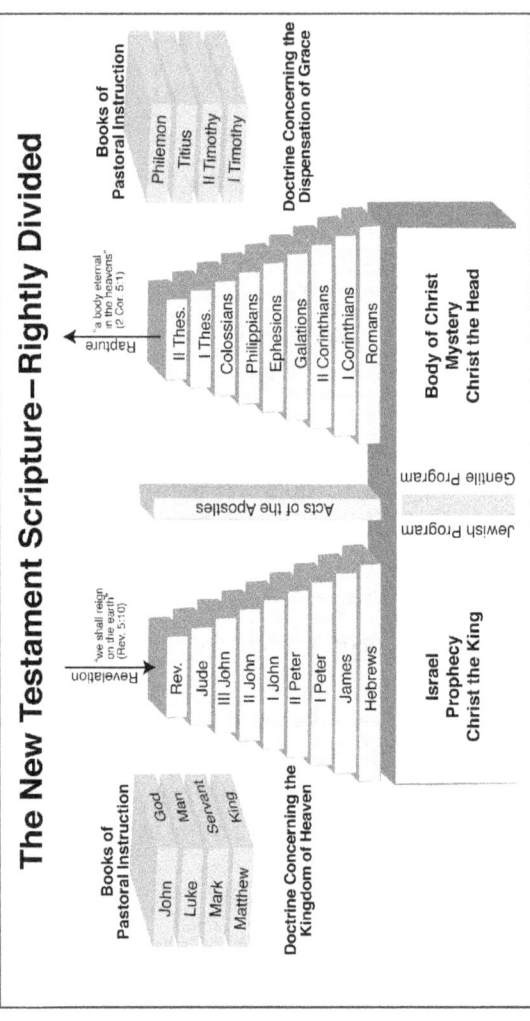

Table 4 The Word rightly Divided	Prophecy	Mystery
Purpose	That Christ reign on earth (Zech. 9:9-11)	That Christ preeminent in all things (Col. 1:18)
Goal	A Kingdom on Earth (Jer. 23:5)	A Body reigning in heaven (2Cor. 5:1; 2Tim. 2:10-12; Eph. 1:23)
Elect Agency	Redeemed Israel (Ex. 19:5 & 6; 1Pet. 2:9)	The Body of Christ (Col. 1:18, 24)
Relationship to Christ	Christ the King (Isa. 9: 6 & 7)	Christ its the Head of the Body (Eph. 1:21-23; 5:23)
Blessings to the Gentiles	Through Israel's rise (Gen. 22:18; 26:3 &4)	Through Israel's fall (Acts 28: 27-28; Rom. 11:11-15)
Relationship of Jew and Gentile	Israel Supreme (Isa. 60:1 – 3)	Jew and Gentile on the same level (Rom. 3:9; 10:12; cf. 11:30-32; Eph. 2:16-17)
View of Nations	Mainly concerns nation (Isa. 2:4. Ezek. 37:21 – 22)	Concerned with individuals (Rom. 10:12 – 13; 2Cor. 5:14 – 17)
The nature of Blessings to Men	Blessings both Physical and Spiritual on earth (Isa. 2:3; 11:1-9)	All Spiritual Blessings in Heavenly Places in Christ (Eph. 1:3-13; Col. 3:1-3)
View of the Lord's presence on earth	Concern's Christ's presence on earth (Isa. 59:20; Zech. 14:4)	Explains His present absence from the earth (Eph. 1:18-23)
Means of Salvation	Faith demonstrated by works (James 2:14-22)	Through Faith alone (Rom. 3:21 – 26; 4:4 & 5; Eph. 2: 8 & 9)
Relation to the Law of Moses	The Law remains in effect (Mat. 28:20 cf. 23:2; Acts 21:20)	The Law taken out of the way (Eph. 2:14-16; Col. 2:14)
Structure	Concerns God's Nation in the earth (Dan. 2:44; Mat. 6:10)	Concerns a body – a living organism (1Cor. 12:12 & 13; Eph. 4:12 – 16)
Miraculous signs and wonders	Required as evidence of faith (Mark 16:16)	Replaced with unfeigned love (1Cor. 13:8)
Apostleship	Twelve apostles, 12 thrones, 12 tribes (Mat. 19:28)	One apostle to one body (Rom. 11:13; Gal. 2: 8 & 9; Eph. 3:1-13)
Commission	Preach and baptize (Mat. 28:19; Mark 16:16)	Preach without Water baptism (1Cor. 1:17; 2Cor. 5:19 – 21; 1Cor. 12:13 cf. Eph. 4:5)
View of the Lord's Return	His return to the earth to Reign (Acts 1:11 cf. 2:36)	Return to the air to catch the Body of Christ away (1Thess. 4:17)

APPENDIX 3 HISTORY TO PROPHECY

| For by him were all things created (Col. 1:16)
He is before all things, and by Him all things consist | All things subdued unto Him (I Cor. 15:27)
All things gathered together in Christ (Eph. 1:10) |

The Creation of Heaven and Earth (Gen 1:1)

The first rebellion – Satan and angels (Isa 14:28; Ezek. 28:140
The first judgment – chaos (Gen 1:2)

The Earth made ready for man (Gen 1:3-31)

The first man and his Bride (Gen 2:18-25)

The subjection to Satan (Gen 3:1-19)

The Earliest Gospel (Gen 3:15)
Universal rebellion (Gen 6:1-7)
Judgment by water (Noah –Gen 6:8-22)
The earth purged by water (Gen 7:17-24)
Governments setup (Gen 9:5-7)

Institution of Babylon
Idolatry invented (Gen 11:1-4)
Nations scattered (Gen 11:5-9)

Call of Israel (Gen 12:1 thru Duet.)
Blessing on Israel (I and II Sam)
Declension in Israel (I & II Kings)
Judgment on Israel (Isaiah, Jer. Ezek.)

The times of the Gentiles begins (Dan, Ezra, Neh.)

The first advent of Christ to the manger

Ministry of Christ
    The Truth
    His rejection and death
    His resurrection and ascension

The Spirit poured out (Acts 2:17)
Second coming in view
The fall of Israel

The Mystery revealed (Eph 3)
The Body called out (Eph 2:11-18)
Gentiles brought in (Rom 11:16-25)

(Center vertical column:) Declaring the end from ancient times (Isaiah 46:20) / I have declared the former things from the beginning (Isaiah 48:3) / In the latter days ye shall consider it perfectly (Jer. 23:20) / I have showed thee new things from this time (Isaiah 48:6)

(Left margin:) History – God's record of the past

(Right margin:) Prophecy – God's story of the future

The New Heaven and New Earth (Rev 21:1)

The final rebellion – Satan and men
The final judgment – fire (Rev 21:8)

The Earth a perfect habitat for man (Rev 22:1-7)

The last Man and His Bride (Rev 21:9-21)

The subjecting of Satan (Rev 20:10)

The Everlasting Gospel (Rev 14:6)
Universal rebellion (Rev 20:8)
Judgment by fire (2Pet 3:7)
The floor purged (Mat 3:12)
Kingdom setup Perfect Government

Destruction of Babylon (Rev. 18:2)
Idolatry ended Rev 9:20; 21:8)
Nations gathered (Rev 16:4; 20:8)

Restoration of Israel (Rev 5:10)
Judgment of tribulation
Repentance of the nation (Rev 7:4)
Blessing of the nation (Rev 21)

The times of the Gentiles ends (Lk 21:24; Rev. 11:5)

The second advent of Christ to the throne

Ministry of Anti-Christ
    The Lie
    His reception and reign
    His destruction and doom

The Spirit again poured out (Rev 19:10; 22:17)
Second coming in view
Rise of Israel

The Mystery ended with the rapture (2Thes 2:7)
The Body caught up (2Thess 4:15)
Gentiles cut off (Rom 11:26)

APPENDIX 4 - SO WHO WROTE HEBREWS?

We understand that God is the author of the book as He is for all of scripture. The question actually is who is the human author of the Book of Hebrews? Perhaps the better question to answer for starters is who did not write the letter. Whoever wrote it shared the same hope that the target audience did (see Appendix 1 on the target audience) – that hope being the coming kingdom established on earth through Christ through Israel under the New Covenant. Paul had committed the unpardonable sin of blaspheming the Holy Ghost as did the unbelieving nation at large. As a result, he had no hope in Israel's program anymore. We conclude that the reference Paul makes about being separated from his mother's womb in Galatians 1:5 is a statement that he no longer had any hope in Israel's program. The following is a study on Acts 9:1-9 regarding the unpardonable sin that Israel as a nation along with Saul of Tarsus had committed.

> "¹ And Saul, yet breathing out threatenings and slaughter against the disciples of the Lord, went unto the high priest, ² And desired of him letters to Damascus to the synagogues, that if he found any of this way, whether they were men or women, he might bring them bound unto Jerusalem. ³ And as he journeyed, he came near Damascus: and suddenly there shined round about him a light from heaven: ⁴ And he fell to the earth, and heard a voice saying unto him, Saul, Saul, why persecutest thou me? ⁵ And he said, Who art thou, Lord? And the Lord said, I am Jesus whom thou persecutest: *it is* hard for thee to kick against the pricks. ⁶ And he trembling and astonished said, Lord, what wilt thou have me to do? And the Lord *said* unto him, Arise, and go into the city, and it shall be told thee what thou must do. ⁷ And the men which journeyed with him stood speechless, hearing a voice, but seeing no man. ⁸ And Saul arose from the earth; and when his eyes were opened, he saw no man: but they led him by the hand, and brought *him* into Damascus. ⁹ And he was three days without sight, and neither did eat nor drink." Acts 9:1-9

This event (the saving of Saul of Tarsus) raises two important questions: 1) When did the Dispensation of the Grace of God begin? and 2) When did the Body of Christ begin? We understand that the dispensation of grace was a mystery hid in God until the time was right for its revelation (Eph. 3:1-4). Saul of Tarsus had committed the unpardonable sin of Matthew 12:31. He could not be forgiven in that world (the age of the Lord's earthly ministry) nor in the world to come (which would be Pentecost when the gospel of the kingdom is proclaimed without the king being present). Paul however did get saved in spite of the fact that he blasphemed the Holy Ghost in not believing the witness of the twelve apostles as the Holy Ghost did the miraculous things through them. The only way for him to be forgiven and be saved was for there to be a new dispensation introduced in which there was no unpardonable sin.

Paul refers to his salvation as one born out of due season (1Cor. 15:8). He was not born in Israel in what was Israel's "Acceptable Year" (Isa. 61:2 cf Luke 4:19). He could not be saved in the 70th week of Daniel when "all Israel shall be saved" (Rom. 11:11:26) for that has now been postponed. We therefore understand that the dispensation of grace started with the saving of Saul of Tarsus. The information concerning the dispensation of grace will be revealed later through Saul who becomes Paul the apostle of the Gentiles (Eph. 3:1-5; Rom. 11:13).

The church which is Christ's Body began when God started forming the Body of Christ – the "one new man" of Ephesians 2:15. Jesus Christ is the first member of this one new man in that He is personally the head of the new creature (2Cor. 5:17). Paul is the first member of the church which is the body of Christ in that he is the pattern of how anyone since then is saved (1Tim. 1:16).

"¹² And I thank Christ Jesus our Lord, who hath enabled me, for that he counted me faithful, putting me into the ministry; ¹³ Who was before a blasphemer, and a persecutor, and injurious: but I obtained mercy, because I did *it* ignorantly in unbelief. ¹⁴ And the grace of our Lord was exceeding abundant with faith and love which is in Christ Jesus.

¹⁵ This *is* a faithful saying, and worthy of all acceptation, that Christ Jesus came into the world to save sinners; of whom I am chief. ¹⁶ Howbeit for this cause I obtained mercy, that in me first Jesus Christ might shew forth all longsuffering, for a pattern to them which should hereafter believe on him to life everlasting. ¹⁷ Now unto the King eternal, immortal, invisible, the only wise God, *be* honour and glory for ever and ever. Amen."

(1 Timothy 1:12-17)

In his book "*The Coming Prince*" Sir Robert Anderson points out that the 69th week of Daniel ended when the Lord rode into Jerusalem on a donkey. As we study Daniel 9 we note that there was a break in the action between the end of the 69th week and the beginning of the 70th (see the underlined passage below). In one of His parables, the Lord gives us the information on how long of a time span that break encompasses (Luke 13:8). Jesus Christ the head together with the church which is His body comprises what the apostle Paul calls "the preaching of Jesus Christ according to the revelation of the mystery (or the "one new man" of Eph. 2:15). The mystery is a special relationship between Jesus Christ and the church which is His Body. The Holy Ghost forms the one new man by baptizing individual members into the body, forming an eternal union of sinners saved by grace apart from human merit with Jesus Christ the Savior.

"²⁵ Know therefore and understand, *that* from the going forth of the commandment to restore and to build Jerusalem unto the Messiah the Prince *shall be* seven weeks, and threescore and two weeks: the street shall be built again, and the wall, even in troublous times. ²⁶ <u>And after threescore and two weeks shall Messiah be cut off, but not for himself: and the people of the prince that shall come shall destroy the city and the sanctuary; and the end thereof *shall be* with a flood, and unto the end of the war desolations are determined.</u> ²⁷ And he shall confirm the covenant with many for one week: and in the midst of the week he shall cause the sacrifice and the oblation to cease, and for the overspreading of abominations he shall make *it* desolate, even until the consummation, and that determined shall be poured upon the desolate." (Daniel 9:25-27)

We see in Luke 13:8 that the Lord added one year between the end of the 69th week and the beginning of the 70th. This event (the saving of Saul) fits this time frame. Stephen (as we saw earlier) was the messenger that Israel sent saying that they will not have Christ reign over them (Luke 19:14). With the stoning of Stephen, Israel as a nation joined the Gentiles in rejection of Christ. The Gentiles had rejected God's reign over them back in Genesis 11. Now Israel joins them in rebellion. The 2nd Psalm tells us what God's response will be to that action. He will speak to them in His wrath and vex them in His sore displeasure. Now we understand that the 70th week of Daniel is going to be the time in which the wrath of God will be poured out on the Christ-rejecting world. At the time of the saving of Saul of Tarsus, the wrath was ready to be poured out. But God had a secret to be revealed. Instead of pouring out His wrath, He saved the leader of the rebellion and sent him to the world with the gospel of the grace of God. Romans 11:32-33 sums up the marvel and the wonder of it all "For God hath concluded them all in unbelief, that he might have mercy upon all. O the depth of the riches both of the wisdom and knowledge of God! How unsearchable *are* his judgments, and his ways past finding out!"

The Twofold Ministry of Paul:

Though it seems clear from this that Paul was not the human author of this book, it is also apparent that the doctrine regarding the atoning work of Christ on the cross that we find in the Book of Hebrews is Pauline. Though Paul did not write the book, would it be that whoever did write it had gotten the doctrine from Paul? The following is an excerpt from the book *More than Conquerors* by M J Tiry (Westbow Press 2019). It shows that there were two items of doctrine that were revealed by our Lord Jesus Christ through Paul. One was the final capstone of revelation concerning what would be accomplished by the cross. This would have a bearing on both the mystery concerning the Body of Christ and the believing remnant of Israel. That mystery of the gospel was kept secret and not revealed at all until it was revealed through Paul and also on the gospel concerning the seed of the woman back in Genesis 3:15 which (according to Romans 1:1) God had promised afore in the holy scriptures.

Romans 1:1 "Paul, a servant of Jesus Christ, called *to be* an apostle, separated unto the gospel of God,…"

Paul, the apostle of the Gentiles (Rom. 11:13) is the writer of the epistle to the Romans. Paul calls himself a servant of Jesus Christ in 2Timothy 1:3. Paul says that he served God from his forefathers "with a pure conscience…", yet he refers to himself as having been a "blasphemer and a persecutor and injurious…" (1Tim. 1:13) but then goes to say "but I obtained mercy because I did it ignorantly in unbelief." We would conclude that his conscience was pure because he was operating on the basis of ignorance. This is the condition of the people our Lord defended in (John 16:2). "They shall put you out of the synagogues: yea, the time cometh, that whosoever killeth you will think that he doeth God service." Saul of Tarsus thought he was doing service to God in persecuting the believers in Jerusalem. A study of our Lord's parable in Matthew 21:33-38 makes it clear that this was not the condition of the leaders of Israel. That is the parable of the householder who had a vineyard that he placed in the hands of husbandmen which we understand to be the leaders of Israel. Verse 38 of that passage tells the story: "³⁸ But when the husbandmen saw the son, they said among themselves, This is the heir; come, let us kill him, and let us seize on his inheritance." Acts 4:13-30 indicates that those same leaders of Israel took knowledge of the disciples after our Lord's resurrection that they (the disciples) had been with the resurrected Lord. They knew Jesus was the Christ but were not willing to let him have what was rightfully his. Had that been Paul's case, he would have not obtained mercy.

According to Romans 1:1, Paul is called to be an apostle. He is a special apostle being uniquely "the apostle of the Gentiles" (Rom. 11:13). As such, he was given the apostleship of the Uncircumcision (Gal. 2: 6-8). Paul's apostleship involved making known the work that Jesus Christ did as "…one mediator between God and men, the man Christ Jesus; Who gave himself a ransom for all, to be testified in due time. Whereunto I am ordained a preacher, and an apostle, (I speak the truth in Christ, and lie not;) a teacher of the Gentiles in faith and verity" (1Tim. 2:5-7). There are twelve apostles who are going to sit on the twelve thrones in the kingdom of Heaven judging the twelve tribes of Israel (Matt. 19:28). Matthias was selected to fill the place on that board (Acts 1:16-26) vacated by Judas.

Paul was "separated unto the gospel of God, (which he had promised afore by his prophets in the Holy Scriptures.)" This is the first verse of Romans. This might seem to contradict the closing verses of Romans. Note Romans 16:25-26:

> "Now to him that is of power to stablish you according to my gospel, and the preaching of Jesus Christ, according to the revelation of the mystery, which was kept secret since the world began, But now is made manifest, and by the scriptures of the prophets, according to the commandment of the everlasting God, made known to all nations for the obedience of faith:"(Romans 16:25-26)

Paul talks about two things in this passage. He speaks of "my gospel" and also he talks about "the preaching of Jesus Christ according to the revelation of the mystery." Paul also speaks of this mystery in Ephesians 3:2-6.

> "If ye have heard of the dispensation of the grace of God which is given me to you-ward: How that by revelation he made known unto me the mystery; (as I wrote afore in few words, Whereby, when ye read, ye may understand my knowledge in the mystery of Christ) Which in other ages was not made known unto the sons of men, as it is now revealed unto his holy apostles and prophets by the Spirit; That the Gentiles should be fellow heirs, and of the same body, and partakers of his promise in Christ by the gospel:"
>
> (Ephesians 3:2-6)

Note:
- The subject of the mystery is the one body (Eph. 3:6).
- The ministry of the mystery is given to Paul (Eph. 3:7-8).
- The operation of the mystery is fellowship (Eph. 3:9).
- The divine purpose for it is to show the wisdom of God (Eph. 3:10).

Back now to Romans 1:1 we see what appears to be a contradiction. Realizing that there are no contradictions in the Bible, we look for the solution to this dilemma where by Paul says he is "separated onto the gospel of God which he [God] had promised afore by his prophets" in Romans 1:1 and tells about the mystery which was "kept secret" and "in other ages not made known."

The solution to what appears to be a contradiction between Romans 1:1-4 and Romans 16:25 is to recognize that Paul is talking about two different things in Romans 16:25 when he speaks of "my gospel" and "the preaching of Jesus Christ according to the revelation of the mystery." What Paul called "my gospel" in 16:25 is what he calls "the gospel of God" in Romans 1:1. This is the gospel that was spoken by God in Genesis 3:15 regarding the "seed of the woman" which would one day crush Satan's head. The means by which, the seed of the woman would do that was not revealed until after it was accomplished. It was the work of the Lord Jesus Christ on the cross that totally defeated Satan. This fact was first made known through Paul as "the mystery of the Gospel" (Eph. 6:19). Paul therefore calls it "the gospel of Christ" (Rom. 1:16) and "my gospel" (Rom. 2:16). What was accomplished by our Savior on the cross had to be kept a secret or it would not have been allowed by te princes of this world to be accomplished (1Cor. 2:6-10). What was accomplished on the cross is actually presented for the first time in the Bible in Romans 3:21-28. 1Corinthians 15:3-4 states it simply.

> "[3] For I delivered unto you first of all that which I also received, how that Christ died for our sins according to the scriptures; [4] And that he was buried, and that he rose again the third day according to the scriptures..."
> (1 Corinthians 15:3-4)

What Paul calls "thy mystery" involves God calling out a body of believers from the Gentiles (fallen Israel included -- Romans 11:32). Israel as a fallen nation is regarded by God as just another Gentile nation today and will be until the dispensation of grace ends with the rapture of the church which is Christ's Body called "the church which is his body" (Col. 1:24). No Old Testament prophet spoke any thing about this mystery because it was "hid in God" (Eph. 3:9) from the beginning of the world until it was revealed through Paul.

The gospel that was "promised" by the prophets was not made known to the prophets (Isa. 64:4 cf. 1Cor. 2:6-10). "What eye had not seen nor ear heard nor entered into the heart of men" in Isaiah 64:4 is now made known to us in Paul's epistles (1Cor. 2:6-10). If you asked Paul what the gospel is he would give you 1Corinthians 15: 3-4. But the twelve during our Lord's earthy ministry and at Pentecost did not tell anyone that because they did not know it yet. The 12 preached "gospel" (Luke 9:6) but what would be accomplished on the cross whereby the shed blood of Christ would be the price of redemption of mankind was still hid from them (Luke 9:45 and 18:34).

The message preached by Peter and the twelve at Pentecost did not include the cross as good news (Acts 2:38). Peter preached the cross but he did not preach it as good news. A careful study Peter's second address at Pentecost (Acts 3:12-26) is revealing in the regard what they understood about the cross. Salvation there was through "Faith in His name" (Acts 3:16). Peter preached the cross as something that had to happen because it was prophesied (Acts 3:18). The formula for salvation in his message in the Book of Acts was repentance for having crucified their Messiah (Acts 2:38 and 3:19).

> Romans 1:2 "(Which he had promised afore by his prophets in the holy scriptures,) 3 Concerning his Son Jesus Christ our Lord, which was made of the seed of David according to the flesh; 4 And declared *to be* the Son of God with power, according to the spirit of holiness, by the resurrection from the dead:..."

Jesus Christ our Lord was made of the seed of David according to the flesh. This refers to his earthly ministry to Israel under the gospel of the kingdom which the twelve preached. This gospel included:

1) A king as Jeremiah 23:15 says "Behold, the days come, saith the LORD, that I will raise unto David a righteous Branch, and a King shall reign and prosper, and shall execute judgment and justice in the earth."
2) A kingdom as Daniel 2:44 "And in the days of these kings shall the God of heaven set up a kingdom..."
Our Lord ministered this gospel to Israel.

- Matthew 4:23 "And Jesus went about all Galilee teaching....their synagogues and preaching the gospel of the kingdom" This will be the tribulation message.
- Matthew 24:14 "And this gospel of the kingdom shall be preached in all the world for a witness unto all nations..." This will ultimately be fulfilled.
- Revelation 11:15 "The seventh angel sounded..."The kingdoms of this world are become the kingdoms of our Lord and of his Christ."

Though our Lord did many miracles and demonstrated his power during his ministry here on earth his power was not fully demonstrated until His resurrection from the dead. Ephesians 1: 19-23 talks about that power that was made manifest by His resurrection "And what is the exceeding greatness of his power to us-ward who believe, according to the working of his mighty power, Which he wrought in Christ, when he raised him from the dead, and set him at his own right hand in the heavenly places, Far above all principality, and power, and might, and dominion, and every name that is named, not only in this world, but also in that which is to come: And hath put all things under his feet, and gave him to be the head over all things to the church Which is his body, the fullness of him that filleth all in all."

Hebrews 5:5 and 6 refers to our Lord's resurrection as the day he was begotten as the Son (Psalm 2:7, Acts 13:33, Heb. 1:5). He was begotten of God when he was conceived in the Virgin Mary's womb (Luke 1:35) but He is declared to be the Son of God with power by his resurrection. As a result, he will be pre-eminent from eternity past to eternity future (2Tim. 1: 9 and Eph. 1:10) and from things under the earth to things far above all heavens (Phil. 2:20). As a result of his resurrection, He could tell His apostles "all power is given unto me in heaven and in earth." (Matt. 28:18)

> "5 By whom we have received grace and apostleship, for obedience to the faith among all nations, for his name: 6 Among whom are ye also the called of Jesus Christ: 7 To all that be in Rome, beloved of God, called *to be* saints: Grace to you and peace from God our Father, and the Lord Jesus Christ." (Romans 1:5-7)
Who are the "we" of Verse five of Romans 1 and who are the "ye" of Verse six? Verse five speaks of Paul

and his companions Timothy, Luke, Jason, and Sosipater (Rom. 16:21) along with Tertius the gramateus (16:22). The apostleship, which is spoken of is that of Paul and Timothy (Paul's yokefellow). The "ye" of Verse 6 speaks to the saints of Rome who received salvation and were called to be saints because of their "obedience of faith."

The term "for the obedience of faith among all nations" is significant here in Verse 5 because our Lord's earthly Ministry was only to the "lost sheep of the house of Israel" (Matt 10:6, 15:24, Rom 15:8). The Ministry of Paul now extends the door of faith to all nations.

Conclusion to Appendix 4

We conclude that Paul was not the human author of Hebrews but whoever did write the book got the doctrine concerning how the merits of the cross applies to the Hebrew people in the Book of Hebrews from Paul. But we ask: "Who is the human author?"

Whoever wrote it was a member of what Paul called the circumcision because the writer shares the kingdom hope of Israel with the audience. So too the writer was associated with Timothy in a prison setting in Italy. I offer for consideration some possibilities here.

- Mark could be a candidate. He is the son of Barnabas's sister who started out traveling with Paul and Barnabas on their first journey but defected from the work. Later however, Paul sends for Mark at the very close of his ministry (2Tim. 4:11) telling Timothy "Take Mark and bring him with thee: for he is profitable to me for the ministry. However, as one compares the writing style of the Gospel of Mark with that of Hebrews, we conclude that it certainly is not the same.

- Luke would be a candidate if he were a member of the circumcision. His writing style as we read Luke's Gospel account does fit the style of Hebrews. However, the fact that Luke is not listed with the circumcision members of Paul's company (Col. 4:11) makes it suspect as to whether or not he is a member of the circumcision. However in the account of Acts 21:17 through 29 we see the Jews concerned that Paul had brought Trophimus (a Gentile) into the temple but had no such concern about Luke. Luke could be a likely suspect as the human author of the Book of Hebrews.

- Another likely candidate as the human author of the book is Apollos who we find first in Acts 18:24. It is said of him that he was a Jew from Alexandra and "This man was instructed in the way of the Lord; and being fervent in the spirit, he spake and taught diligently the things of the Lord, knowing only the baptism of John. And he began to speak boldly in the synagogue: whom when Aquila and Priscilla had heard, they took him unto *them*, and expounded unto him the way of God more perfectly." (Acts 18:25-26) Apollos was a circumcision believer preaching the hope of Israel for that was what the baptism of John was all about. After being instructed in the Pauline message of what was accomplished on the cross he began to ministry with Paul much like how Barnabas (another circumcision believer) did. It is therefore my considered opinion that Apollos is the human author of the Book of Hebrews but I leave it to you to decide for yourself. Whether you agree or disagree, let's remember that the first word of the book tells us who the real author of the Book of Hebrews is (as God is the real author of all of scripture).

A Study in Hebrews
Israel and the New Covenant

The Book of Hebrews is regarded by many as the most eloquently written piece of literature. It sits in the cannon of Scripture as the first of what we call "the Circumcision Epistles." These "Circumcision Epistles" (Hebrews through the Revelation) will take Israel "on to perfection" in their redemptive program. These circumcision epistles will give redeemed Israel all of the information that they will need to get through the coming Tribulation Period and into the promised Kingdom of Heaven. It is the foundational book regarding the atoning work of Jesus Christ in the context of God's redemption of Israel. The Book of Hebrews will provide for the Jewish people who will be going through the coming tribulation period what the Book of Romans does for us who live in this present "dispensation of grace." It presents that nation the merits of the cross and the shed blood of Jesus Christ as the price of redemption.

Three key points of doctrine are found in Hebrews pertaining to that nation. They are: 1) the atoning work of Jesus Christ as Israel's High Priest who went into the real tabernacle in heaven. He did this not with the blood of bulls and goats as did the high priests of the Old Testament under the Old Covenant, but with His own blood to obtain eternal redemption for the nation. 2) As the nation's High Priest, He will initiate the New Covenant for the nation to equip that nation to be the blessing to the Gentiles nations that God intended it to be in the beginning. 3) Thirdly, the book of Hebrews presents a series of warnings that stress the importance of enduring the chastening that will come on the nation because Israel is God's Son.

ABOUT THE AUTHOR

Michael J. Tiry came to know the Lord Jesus Christ as his personal Savior at the age of twenty-nine while in the midst of a career as an engineer. Michael served in the United States Civil Service as a professional engineer for 25 years. After 25 years with the civil service, Michael also started, owned and operated a private engineering company. While engaged in a career as an engineer, he also was involved with other men in the founding a local Bible believing church. His deep appreciation for having the assurance of eternal life, his passion for study, and his quest for truth compelled him to search deeply into the Bible with a desire to learn its truth that he might present the riches of God's grace to others. Over the last forty five plus years Michael has been involved in itinerant preaching, a church planting ministry, and a teaching and preaching ministry at Berean Bible Church in Chippewa Falls, Wisconsin. Michael also serves Berean Bible Church as director of the Timothy Institute – a Bible curriculum designed to prepare men for leadership in local churches. Additionally, Mike has been active over a span of twenty three years in a prison ministry. Michael and his wife (Linda) of forty five years have raised five daughters.

OTHER BOOKS BY THE SAME AUTHOR

Michael has written over sixteen books which are used as study guides in the Timothy Institute. This book is one of the three that has been published. Others include "*You and Your Creator*," "A Study in *Genesis from Adam to Abraham*," and "*More than Conquerors* (recently republished as "*Super Abounding Grace*")." All are available through Amazon, Barnes and Noble and other book distributors.